21. 8. 2018

# READER'S DIGEST & THE ROYALS

# READER'S DIGEST
# & THE ROYALS

## A jubilee celebration of the British royal family
### *from the magazine archives*

*PUBLISHED BY*
*The Reader's Digest Association, Inc.*
*London • New York • Sydney • Montreal*

# Contents

# Foreword

Attitudes to the monarchy have undergone something of a revolution in the sixty years that Elizabeth has been our Queen. The age of deference has passed, the royal family are held to account and the modern media leave them with few places to hide. But, through all this, support for the monarchy has hardly wavered from a highly respectable 70 per cent plus, and the Queen herself remains constant. The very fact that, for most of us, she has simply been there in the background for all our lives provides a valuable continuity and stability both in the United Kingdom and the Commonwealth.

This absorbing selection of articles about the Queen and her family through the past six decades gives a graphic illustration of just how much things have changed. It's astonishing now to think that the young Queen and her husband spent six months travelling the world in 1954, leaving their two small children behind. One American contributor called it "the most successful piece of public relations ever attempted". It's also fascinating to see how language has altered over the years: these days no-one is likely to write "the Queen acknowledged the RAF salute with a gay wave"!

There are thoughtful portraits of Prince Charles as he approached his 21st birthday ("a decent, ordinary sort of chap"), and of the Queen Mother at 75 (full of mischief and warmth). But it's the analysis of the Queen's role at pivotal points in her reign – such as the Silver Jubilee or her fortieth year on the throne – that provides the most insight into the woman we all know of, but few can claim to know. After some twenty years of reporting on the monarchy, I concur with the view of a faithful old servant quoted in one of these articles: that the Queen is a "nicer, funnier person than is often realised".

And what better way to acknowledge that than with this affectionate Diamond Jubilee tribute to her long and successful reign?

*Jennie Bond*
*May 2012*

# INTRODUCTION

When DeWitt Wallace, a young American soldier, was recovering from shrapnel wounds sustained during World War I, he spent much of his convalescence reading articles from a huge range of magazines. He wanted to continue that breadth of reading once he'd recovered. But how on earth would he—or, indeed, any other reader—find the time?

His answer appeared in 1922 with the launch issue of *Reader's Digest*, featuring condensed versions of articles of "enduring value and interest". Sixteen years later, in 1938, the magazine was launched in the UK—the first of many international editions. *Reader's Digest* rapidly became a global publishing phenomenon, and is now published in 50 countries and 21 different languages—the world's biggest (and almost certainly best-loved!) magazine.

But be warned: start reading through our back issues, and it's hard to stop. They offer a riveting social history, full of fascinating insights spanning nearly three-quarters of a century.

No surprise then, given our long history, that the royal family have made regular appearances in the magazine (most recently with our behind-the-scenes look at the wedding of Prince William and Catherine Middleton). Following the royals' progress gives a glimpse not just of the way they were, but the way we were, too.

From the outset, *Reader's Digest* was a strong supporter of new Queen as she set sail, aged just 28, to reach out to her people around the world. For some countries, this was the first time they'd ever seen their sovereign—and this fresh-faced young Queen, with her unshakeable devotion to duty, won them over with ease.

What I like most about the contemporary accounts—of family life as well as all the pomp and ceremony—are the small-but-telling observations. A 1957 article, for example, comments on the Queen's facial expression: "Without the Smile, relationship between girl-at-desk and the ancestors-on-wall is quickly apparent…this stern-mouthed Hanoverian heritage has been a trial since childhood". Or there's the Queen Mother, dancing with a "nervous and fumble-footed student at a university ball", who encourages him by saying, "Cheer up…You haven't knocked my tiara off—yet!"

But over the years we've done more than simply report on the royals. In 1986, for example, *Reader's Digest* commissioned a portrait of the Queen to mark her sixtieth birthday. The painting, by Michael Leonard, featured on page 8, shows a smiling, seated queen with a Corgi. (It's known affectionately as Corgi and Bess!)

And in 1997 we commissioned another painting, by Tai-Shan Schierenberg, featured on page 157, to celebrate the Queen's golden wedding anniversary.

We even had a letter from the Queen in 1988 to congratulate us on the occasion of our 50th anniversary, highlighting our "successful half-century of responsible and entertaining journalism."

So in this, the Queen's Diamond Jubilee year, it's our pleasure to return the favour by marking her anniversary with this treasure trove of features reproduced from the archives of *Reader's Digest*. Whether you're pro-Monarchy or not, it's hard to disagree with our Royal writer Tim Heald when he said: "The sovereign and the monarchy have lived through… almost constant change in every area, and they have managed to accommodate it while remaining beacons of constancy in an uncertain world. Against all odds [the monarchy] remains intact. The achievement is undeniable." All the more so, given that his comments were made 20 years ago!

***Gill Hudson***
Reader's Digest *magazine Editor-in-Chief*
*May 2012*

BUCKINGHAM PALACE

Mr. Michael Randolph,
Editor-in-Chief,
Reader's Digest.

Thank you for your message of loyal
greetings which you have sent on the
occasion of the 50th anniversary of the
first publication of the British edition
of Reader's Digest. Please convey my
warm appreciation to your colleagues and
your readers.

I congratulate you on a successful
half century of responsible and
entertaining journalism, which has won
your magazine its place as one of the
most widely read journals in the United
Kingdom.

*Elizabeth R*

March, 1988.

*H.M. QUEEN ELIZABETH II*
*Commissioned by Reader's Digest in 1986 to celebrate Her Majesty's sixtieth birthday*
*Artist: Michael Leonard*
*The portrait is on display in the National Portrait Gallery, London*

*Queen Elizabeth in Napier, New Zealand, during the Royal tour*

# Ladies and Gentlemen, the Queen!

## By Robert C. Ruark

POSSIBLY the most ambitious and certainly the most successful piece of public relations ever attempted will just have been completed, when this report reaches print, by a young woman who left her kids at home to go off on a six months' salesmanship job. The kids were in good hands, back home with Granny.

*Queen Elizabeth's monumental trip, says this famous American journalist, proves that the world still dearly loves a Royal symbol*

This young lady, who is pretty and slight and only 28, is Queen Elizabeth II of England; she has just completed a six months' circle of the globe, in order to assure her loyal but distant subjects that things are going well with her, and to give them a look at the first sovereign ever to visit some of their lands. She was assisted in this gruelling job by her husband, the Duke of Edinburgh, her Prince Consort and father of the future King of England.

Never was a more staggering jaunt attempted. The pair covered 50,000 miles and visited 14 countries. They travelled by train, plane, ship, helicopter, jeep, car and horse-carriage. The complete programme for the Royal tour filled a closely written book an inch thick. A year went into the scheduling of the trip; even the Queen's walking time from ship to shore and from plane to car was worked out on a time sheet.

The tour involved a piece of logistics roughly comparable to a small war. The Royal luggage weighed 12 tons, and Army, Navy and Air Forces were deployed in supporting rôles. The Queen had her own personal retinue of ten household servants, with admirals, colonels, majors, ladies-in-waiting dancing in perpetual attendance. But they were still living out of the suitcases, and they never settled down long enough to get the laundry done.

Elizabeth and Philip attended 185 state functions, balls, parties, luncheons and dinners. They planted trees, unveiled memorials, laid wreaths, held investitures, broadcast speeches, opened Parliaments. Between each function they appeared in a free carnival.

By way of diversion—diversion! —Her Majesty and Consort displayed a seemly interest in sheep shearing, cricket, woodchopping, horse racing. They attended plays, ballets, a music festival and 27 displays by children. On the Royal agenda were a couple of Australian mines, a steel mill, a native dance in New Zealand, where she was symbolically attacked by a Maori warrior, and then given a ceremonial club with which to defend herself. In Tonga she sat cross-legged on the ground with the mountainous Queen Salote while eating roast pig with her fingers.

The Royal couple shook about 50,000 hands, changed costumes an average of four times a day, and reviewed countless troops and constabularies. Through it all—as this is written—they never missed a serious engagement or fell seriously ill, maintaining a pace that would have killed an Olympic marathoner. Despite crowds that gave you an

outdoor claustrophobia just to watch them crush each other, they conformed precisely to their schedules.

The top billing for this grand tour —a good portion of which I witnessed in Australia and New Zealand—is a double one, but it seemed to be agreed in the Antipodes that a large part of the success of the trip was due to Philip. The throne of England and its Commonwealth is not ruled by a Queen with a rubber-stamp consort. It is a hard-working operation shared by two people of equal responsibility and ability.

Elizabeth's sense of perfection is as good as that of any star actress. She spent hours on a special face make-up. In Sydney, the lighting system for a big ceremonial dinner clashed with her make-up, her costume, and the seating arrangement. The Queen, looking over the plans, immediately ordered the system to be changed. Learning that winds are high in February and March in Australia, she had the hems of her shorter skirts weighted to thwart any flirtatious breeze.

Her wardrobe, which included scores of long frocks for state gatherings, more than 60 special costumes with shoes and hats, plus 200 pairs of white gloves, never presented her as anything but immaculate. Perhaps the make-up helped, but she never looked drawn or tired. She is a model of long training in studied public deportment. Her walk is superb, her carriage magnificent, and nowadays she is as slim as a wand. Probably the word "radiant," used in every newspaper account, has never been more overworked. It is a natural radiance. But I do know that the Queen is never unconscious of her appearance.

One day, her handsome Australian equerry, Commander Michael Parker, was helping her into a limousine with a plastic dome—which keeps off the rain and still allows the throngs to see Her Majesty. She turned to Parker to say:

"Michael, how do I look?"

"You look like an orchid under cellophane, Your Majesty," Parker replied, and the Queen beamed like a maiden.

That Elizabeth realizes the full import of being Queen was demonstrated in Auckland, New Zealand. At some festivity at the Town Hall, it began to rain. Prime Minister Holland seized a light plastic raincoat from the nearest man at hand and whipped it round the dainty shoulders of his Queen.

Elizabeth smiled and made the faintest suggestion of a curtsy.

"Thank you, Sir Walter Raleigh," she said.

As a critical expert on crowds she never stopped working. On one occasion, in Rotorua, New Zealand, some Maori girls were performing a classic *poi* dance, in which the maidens manipulate little leather balls on the ends of thongs to imitate rowing the great canoes which brought the Maoris on the long voyage from Polynesia to New Zealand. The Duke became fascinated with the subtle juggling, and asked the Prime Minister, Sidney Holland, about it. The P.M. ordered some balls for the Duke's inspection.

As the Duke began to play with them, the crowd's attention veered from the dance to Philip, who was having great fun with his toys. Quickly the Queen turned and as calmly as a mother takes a breakable object from a child, she plucked the leather balls from his hands and directed his attention back to the dance.

The Duke has a homely touch his wife lacks, since she has been trained from birth to do her queenly job, and to do it on schedule, with a marked distaste for departure from what has been arranged. Philip has a habit of lagging behind to talk when he is interested. He held up an entire press reception in Canberra to talk to a correspondent about matters in which he was interested. He likes to laugh and he likes a joke, and takes himself only as seriously as state occasions demand.

But the fact remains that the Queen is the real symbol. Millions thronged to see her. Never in my life have I observed such an emotional impact of an individual on masses of people, or such a solidification of mass loyalty for common weal. Crowds came in from the country and slept in the parks. They ate sandwich lunches and stood in baking heat, in the rain— not for hours, but for days.

They redecorated their homes and bought new outfits. They spent fortunes to dress their cities in bunting and arches and decorated lighting effects. Sydney alone spent nearly £1,500,000 (Australian) to decorate the streets, and shot off 15 *tons* of rockets on the evening of the Queen's arrival. Melbourne probably spent more, out of sheer civic jealousy. The humblest home in Australia had a Royal motif, and was hung with flags.

Through all this—through a tour that started in December, took in Bermuda, Jamaica, Fiji, Tonga, New Zealand, Australia, the Cocos Islands, Ceylon, Aden, Uganda and the Mediterranean, the pair proceeded, smiling, tactful, indulgent and regal, keeping a strict schedule and keeping this thought in mind: *Show the flag. And we are the flag.*

By her stunning performance Elizabeth refuted the critics who attacked her tour, said royalty was getting too expensive, and wasn't worth the £500,000 it cost annually.

The tour has proved, if it needed proof again, that the people of the world dearly worship a symbol, and if the symbol is for good, then the symbol for bad has no chance against it. You cannot be a Communist or a Fascist and stand, with tears streaming down your face, for two days in the sun or rain to catch a fleeting glance of a young girl who wears a crown. Even as an American spectator, with a certain irreverence for royalty, I was deeply moved by what I saw and heard. No Hitler, no Stalin, ever reaped *this* kind of honest and spontaneous adulation.

Maybe it was coolly and skilfully designed public relations; but Britain's No. 1 Public Relations Expert also wept when Prime Minister Menzies said to her in Melbourne: "You are in your own country, among your own people. We are yours—all parties, all creeds."

As an American I should like to say:

"God save their gracious Queen! She is needed by this world."

---

## Sold!

*W*HEN a large firm advertised in the newspapers to fill a vacancy on its sales staff, one applicant replied: "I am at present selling furniture at the address below. You may judge my ability as a salesman if you will call in to see me at any time, pretending that you are interested in buying furniture.

"When you come in, you can identify me by my red hair. And I will have no way of identifying you. Such salesmanship as I exhibit during your visit, therefore, will be no more than my usual workaday approach and not a special effort to impress a prospective employer."

From among more than 1,500 applicants, the redhead got the job.
—Irving Hoffman in *Go*

# When the Queen Came Home . . .

*By Francis and Katharine Drake*

O N THE MORNING of Thursday, May 13, 1954, an R.A.F. patrol plane, 200 miles from land, sighted a small ship, spanking along as though in an exceptional hurry. She showed a mustard-coloured smoke-stack, a white superstructure, and her raked bow pointed towards England. One look sufficed. The fliers broke into cheers, tossed caps around and swooped down to salute the little vessel at deck level. Luck had selected them to be the first of millions of impatient Britons to welcome the royal yacht *Britannia*,

*An eye-witness account by an American couple of the spontaneous and moving welcome that greeted Queen Elizabeth, returning to Britain after her unprecedented journey round the world*

bearing home Her Majesty Queen Elizabeth the Second after a six-month tour round her realm; their enthusiasm gave only a rough idea of what was waiting for Her Majesty at her journey's end.

The Queen, acknowledging the

R.A.F. salute with a gay wave, was unaware that she was heading into a home-coming demonstration unprecedented in British history—an all-out people's welcome, spontaneous, unrehearsed, tumultuous. She knew only that the Home Fleet waited to greet her at Plymouth in the morning, and that her 50,000 miles of travelling would end on Saturday when she arrived in London and drove home in the ceremonial coach. It looked much like the usual routines prescribed for royal returns long centuries ago.

This was one time, however, that the British people ignored routines. Instead of waiting conventionally to wave from London's pavements, they suddenly cast tradition to the winds. They crowded into trains and buses and headed hilariously for the south coast.

By Thursday morning, roads groaned under a load of traffic unsurpassed since D Day—cars, lorries, scooters, cycles, carts — all hurrying to the shore. Over footpaths and byways came hikers with knapsacks. Each hour trains disgorged more and more thousands at coastal key points. Ports and small villages wore the resplendent air of momentarily awaiting the royal presence in the high street. From a thatched roof, perched over Mevagissey Harbour, flew a starched bed sheet, embroidered in red-and-blue cardboard letters. It read: "God Bless You, Dear!"

By noon old people and young, babies, even dogs, were massing on the cliffs. Repasts, spread over endless bluffs and headlands, uncovered an added reason for high spirits. The last of Britain's food controls were ending.

Next day the multitudes camped on Rame Head were rewarded with a thrilling spectacle. Shortly before 9 a.m. the grey curtains shrouding Plymouth to the east parted. Through the opening appeared the dramatic silhouette of the Home Fleet, 17 ships of the line, dressed over-all and headed by *Vanguard*. Behind her, in three faultless columns, came carriers, cruisers, destroyers, frigates—a procession three and a half miles long and two miles wide. The next moment grey curtains lifted in the west. Through them entered the royal yacht, escorted by destroyers. On the saluting bridge stood the Queen and her tall sailor husband.

The flotillas approached each other majestically, grey shapes shearing grey waters, spray flying over long Atlantic swells. Then, abruptly, a hoist of signals snapped at *Vanguard's* yardarm. The guns of the entire Home Fleet thundered in unison. The 21-gun royal salute crashed over the Devon hilltops, reverberating round the world by radio relays. *Britannia* knifed on ruler-straight between the cheers, the gun smoke, the avenue of passing warships. Then came another signal: *"Execute!"* The Home

Fleet reversed course in a superb manœuvre, maintaining exact station, two columns describing a semi-circle to starboard, the third a corresponding swing to port. Great silver-snouted helicopters carried the measure into the third dimension.

It was now decently in order for the Home Fleet, spread out behind *Britannia* like a bridal veil, to get on with the business of escorting her to the Isle of Wight.

"Your Majesty, with humble duty!" invited the flagship. *Britannia* accepted with pleasure and becoming surprise.

"A wonderful moment!" *Britannia* signalled back.

By the Queen's wish, the 100-mile voyage was accomplished "as close inshore as is compatible with safety." As a result, millions of the self-appointed welcoming body obtained a view of the procession. In and out of fog, haze, squalls and showers led the royal route. Contact, shore-to-ship, however, remained unbroken. It was sustained by bands, church bells, cannon, loudspeakers, telescopes and an armada of intrepid small craft.

The whole south coast had become one tremendous grandstand. The welcome built up to an uproarious pitch that a stranger might have thought overdone, almost hysterical. But a stranger could not have known the deep emotions that stirred the British on this day. They were not only welcoming home their hard-working young Queen. They

were celebrating the success of a desperate struggle out of bankruptcy, showing the world a new and vital Britain risen from the ruin of war.

To Elizabeth it was the finest home-coming gift in the world. Signals pouring into the royal yacht told her that production had reached a record level in British history. Interest and sinking fund on the U.S. loan were fully paid. Steel, electricity, food outputs were all making records.

As the royal yacht steamed on, an incident underlined one of the reasons for Elizabeth's popularity. In a bank of mist, the three-man crew of the fishing trawler *Endeavour* suddenly beheld the yacht looming almost above them. A young fisherman named Terry Ekers rushed to the mast, dipped their red ensign in salute. Then he whipped off his cap and froze to attention beside his jerseyed shipmates. Gravely, the Queen gave an order, and the huge white ensign on *Britannia* dipped in acknowledgment as ceremoniously as if replying to an ocean liner. It was no grandstand play. No one ashore could even see it. It was simply that, to the Queen, three fishermen earning their living were as important as the highest in the land. It is for countless such actions, coming from the heart, that Elizabeth's people love her.

The Solent, from which was launched most of the D-Day invasion force, offered the shorebound the first chance for a close-up. To safeguard vantage spots, many had camped overnight in cars, tents, even haystacks, for here it was that the Home Fleet would take leave of the Queen with another dramatic manœuvre—a high-speed mass convergence on *Britannia*, a precision turn-off at 100 yards and a sweep-past, all hands standing by to cheer.

But no sooner did the coast-guard lookout sight *Britannia* than the scene at the Solent turned to pandemonium, a three-ring circus covering air, sea, land. Without warning, aircraft of all descriptions darted into the overcast: private, chartered, single- and multi-engined—diving and churning, no two flying in the same direction. Now R.A.F. flying boats battled to clear a path for an on-coming jet salute. The 60 navy jets streaked through the mêlée like comets, emerging miraculously in the clear. On the water things were in an equal turmoil. Small craft suddenly up-anchored, escaping in all directions — yachts, trawlers, tenders, tugs, excursion steamers, dinghies, dories. They cut loose with a disregard for danger unequalled since Dunkirk. They ducked inside warship screens, disappeared in wakes, popped up again like corks, waved arms, oars, lifebelts, rushing *Britannia* from every angle. Commands blinked from warships: *"Little Ships Move Over!"; "Keep Off!"*

The destroyer *Duchess* finally saved the day. Breaking escort, she improvised a zigzag dance before the royal yacht, barking out paralysing threats through her loudspeakers. She cleared a path just wide enough for the Home Fleet's final ritual, another masterpiece of seamanship. The 17 great ships tore by, crews lining rails, *Vanguard's* band playing: "God Save the Queen!" As the Queen smiled and waved, the Home Fleet headed once more to sea.

*Britannia* was nearing Portsmouth when, from nowhere, appeared a long green barge. It passed unchallenged through warship screens and aimed for the royal yacht. In the cockpit sat a venerable figure, wearing a baggy reefer jacket, a jaunty cap and chewing a long cigar.

A lot of thoughts had turned to him that day. The sight of concrete tank traps, still barricading the shore, had stirred up memories of a less happy occasion in British history, of a beleaguered island confronting an overwhelming foe. Thousands had caught again an echo of words which had inspired everybody's courage, had cast out doubt and dared the enemy to cross this very strip of water: "We shall fight on the beaches . . . on the landing grounds . . . in the fields and in the streets . . . in the hills. . . . *We shall never surrender. . . .*"

*Britannia's* engines slowed. She lowered her starboard gangway, reserved exclusively for royalty. Amid bedlam, the valiant old warrior pitched his cigar away and climbed aboard. By unprecedented honour,

Sir Winston Churchill, first servant of the realm, accompanied his Queen on the last stretch of her triumphant journey home.

By midnight, thousands were re-enacting south-coast picnic scenes on London's rainy parapets and pavements, determined to see the Queen next day from a front row. Old and young reclined, squatted, huddled, supervised by fatherly policemen. Rain, driven by east winds, came down in cloudbursts.

By morning it let up. High over the crowds that lined the route to Buckingham Palace appeared 30-foot standards, crowned with lions and unicorns, supporting decorative shields which commemorated the different areas of Her Majesty's tour. Down on the exposed Embankment (where, at 3.30 p.m., the Queen would land) and on Westminster Bridge winds lashed the shivering crowds.

WHILE LONDON waited, *Britannia* made her way round the cliffs of Dover and into the Thames estuary. Today marked the first time that any sovereign had re-entered the kingdom by the gloomy old waterway that had helped to build an Empire. River traffic was at a standstill, and the 50-mile tideway presented an unforgettable panorama. The Thames "home fleet," grubby hulls spectacularly "dressed," was lined up two and three deep—coasters, canal barges, tugs, tankers and stubby freighters.

*Britannia* sailed gravely between avenues of dipping jib arms, wharf cranes, salutes from warehouse hooters and ships' sirens and cheering carpets of humanity. She sailed past sites and scenes woven into British history—the old Fort at Tilbury where Elizabeth I had defied the oncoming Spaniards, past Deptford Reach, where, nearly four centuries before, Francis Drake anchored his galleon, *The Golden Hind*, after her voyage round an almost unknown world, where he knelt on her weathered deck to receive his knighthood.

Now appeared a barge, slowly and ceremoniously rowed. In the stern, attired in black and gold robes of office, stood the Lord Mayor of London. He doffed a mediæval cocked hat and bowed. In words well-chosen many centuries before, speaking for the "free men" of London, he welcomed the Sovereign to the city. The great bascules of Tower Bridge opened wide. *Britannia* passed slowly between the buttresses and dropped anchor in the Pool of London.

BACK ON the Embankment, the 41-gun salute fired by the Tower batteries stirred up fresh paroxysms of excitement. Westminster Bridge, spanned by a solid arch of faces, cheered and let fly with jubilant renditions of "The Bells Are Ringing for Me and My Gal!" A detachment of naval ratings, immaculately pipe-clayed, marched on to the Embankment. The Grenadier Guards arrived, red coats, bearskins, white gloves, preceded by a stirring brass band. They formed themselves into a Guard of Honour. Up clattered the Household Cavalry, plumes waving, breastplates gleaming, black horses set off by saddle pads of snowy bearskin. Personages began to arrive—the Archbishop of Canterbury, lords and their ladies, gold-braided officers ablaze with medals.

And now, round the bend from Whitehall, appeared a Cinderella picture—outriders in scarlet, a royal coach drawn by matched greys, ridden by white-wigged postilions in blue and gold. At 3 p.m. appeared the Prime Minister, who had disembarked from *Britannia* down the river.

A few more minutes and there began a roar, generated by a million human lungs and reinforced by gun-fire, bands, horns, hooters, sirens and a last frenzied chorus of "The Bells Are Ringing!" from the bridge. At long last, the royal barge was coming into view. It nosed round the final bend. The hubbub waned. It sank into the sound of a great sigh. There stood Elizabeth and Philip once again, back where they both belonged, recovered unharmed, unspoiled, unchanged in charm and grace and dignity. They stood beside each other, smiling and waving, looking too young to have to bear the heavy burdens of a Crown. With them stood their two children, Charles and Anne. The

barge advanced towards the landing in a hush. It was as though the people wanted a moment more to hug this picture close.

Then the barge came smartly alongside. The Queen stepped forward. She looked at the great throngs which had come to welcome her, at the possessive smiles, the angular, obstinate, somehow special faces of her people of the motherland. Then her own face broke into a radiant smile and she stepped quickly ashore.

As she did so, every church bell in the land began to peal. Facing Her Majesty stood the battalion of her own Grenadier Guards. On her right the black horses of her Household Cavalry pranced and jingled. In front of them stood the open carriage waiting to take her back to Buckingham Palace.

"Grenadier Guards, pres-*e-e-nt*, *hup!*"

Rifles, with bayonets fixed, flashed in two clock-like motions. The national anthem crashed out from the Guards' band. The two standard-bearers took a pace forward. Slowly, the proud colours of the Regiment were lowered until they lay in the dust before the Queen, the only person in the world to whom this honour may be paid.

Elizabeth stood alone, listening to the tumultuous cheering and the clear bells of Westminster Abbey ringing out her welcome. Not for the first time that day, she was close to tears. At long last, she was home!

VOLUME 71

*The*
Reader's Digest

OCTOBER 1957

© 1957 The Reader's Digest Association, Inc.

An exclusive study of the
most remarkable young woman of our time

*Elizabeth II:*
*the Commonwealth's Queen*

E II R

By Francis and Katharine Drake

A T ADMIRALTY ARCH, outside St. James's Park, a policeman is holding back traffic, extending the right of way to a sprightly little horse-drawn carriage whose maroon door panels display the Royal Arms. Inside the carriage repose some worn, red-leather cases —the Queen's Boxes, containing top-secret reports and memoranda flown in daily from all over the world.

The equipage clip-clops up the Mall, passes a vast statue of great-great-grandmother Queen Victoria, and enters the cobble-stoned Royal Mews of Buckingham Palace. Here a Queen's Messenger descends with the boxes—one of them a top-priority Foreign Office box—and carries them through nearly half a mile of corridors to a room on the second floor of the Palace.

This is a famous room. Virtually inaccessible, guarded jealously, it is the Queen's "office." About 99 per cent living-room, it is spacious and handsome, with a subtle colour-scheme of green and oyster-grey: green walls, grey draperies and carpet, against which the light reflects a rich gleam from period porcelain, crystal, gold-leaf, silver and glossy table-tops. Staring down from the walls, some dozen peruked ancestors, combining looks of melancholy virtue with heavy, full-lipped mouths, share a family resemblance.

This is essentially a feminine room—all that challenges it is a man-sized mahogany desk, right-angled in a huge bay window overlooking the Palace gardens. The desk is awash with official-looking papers, and from it a wall of photographs juts up, a cheerful hotch-potch of children, family groups, uniforms, boats, dogs, horses.

At this desk, pen in hand, brow puckered, is sitting one of the most remarkable young women of our time—Elizabeth II, by the Grace of God, Queen of the United Kingdom, Head of the Commonwealth, Defender of the Faith. But neither hereditary titles nor the documents

before her reflect Elizabeth's personal record of achievement—the fact that in five brief years her effort and personality have made her the best loved, best known, most travelled, most energetically dedicated sovereign in the long history of the realm.

Elizabeth is wearing a cherry-red woollen dress, pearl necklace, pearl ear-rings and no shoes. It is one of the rare moments of the day when the royal footwear can be off-duty, even if their owner cannot. Shorn of familiar tiara, high heels, floor-length gowns, Elizabeth looks younger than her 31 years, smaller even than her measurements: height 5 ft. 4 in., waist 24. There is about her a tissue-paper immaculacy, a formidable neatness. Not a wisp has escaped the moderately wavy, conventionally coiffeured, medium-brown hair; the famous Windsor skin is petal fresh. In private, Elizabeth is as regal as in public—no impatient gestures, no elbows on the desk, no slouching. The royal back is like a board, a legacy from the late Queen Mary.

Now the Queen selects a gold key—there are only two and the Foreign Secretary has the other—and opens the dispatch box. The first missive she picks out is written on White House paper, it is signed "Dwight D. Eisenhower" and contains an invitation to visit the United

---

OPPOSITE : *Her Majesty Queen Elizabeth II by Pietro Annigoni*

States in October 1957, a date then four months off.

The Queen is delighted, but not exactly bowled over by surprise. The invitation has been hanging fire for nearly 18 months. Initiated at low diplomatic levels to avoid boomerang embarrassments, it was finally smiled on by President Eisenhower and the Prime Minister, then shelved because of the Middle East situation, revived for spring possibilities, dropped because of royal commitments to Portugal, France and Denmark, reconsidered, scuttled by indiscreet "leaks," finally revived for the opening of the Canadian Parliament.

The actual appearance of the invitation informs the Queen (*a*) that it has finally achieved the blessing of the three governments, (*b*) that her wish has come true—to visit America during the year commemorating the first British settlement at Jamestown. The plan is of such importance that the Palace will henceforward allude to it as The Visit.

***From Empire into Partnership:*** On the surface, The Visit looks like any other routine trip by royalty. Actually, it is designed to emphasize the coming of age of a new group of nations. Elizabeth goes to visit America less as Queen of England than as *Head of the Commonwealth*, an organization in which Empire domination has been replaced by partnership.

The serious-faced young Queen knows that much water has flowed under London Bridge since 1776, when ancestor George III, up on the wall, lost those tiresome Colonies. To Britons of the Queen's generation, "colonialism" is a dead issue. She is as proud as her countrymen that while the Communists have been holding 100 million foreign people behind the Iron Curtain and giving them the treatment of Hungary, Britain has been freeing 500 million from colonial ties, investing £100 million a year in their local industries, helping them to organize complete self-government, no strings attached.

From daily perusal of her "boxes," Elizabeth also knows that this policy is good for all concerned. Britain's trade with her former territories has nearly doubled, while their own local revenues have increased 1,200 per cent.

The Queen has made herself the symbol of this Commonwealth's unity. With her husband, she has tramped the length and breadth of the new nations, making devoted friends. She has contrived to bring to the hackneyed and often dreary job of royalty a youth and vitality which matches that of the Commonwealth itself. The new nations feel that she understands them. They believe that she is on their side—and to an extraordinary extent, she is. The young Queen and her husband will probably influence the world in which we live as few couples have ever done in history.

What sort of person is this young

woman? Just what is her character? How does she behave? How well does she do her inexpressibly difficult job?

***The Girl and the Queen:*** Sitting alone at her desk, intently considering all the implications of the American invitation, something is missing from the Queen's appearance as the world generally sees it: it is the Smile, target of millions of cameras, the catalyst that can bestow on Elizabeth's fresh good looks a quality of beauty. Without the Smile, relationship between girl-at-desk and the ancestors-on-wall is quickly apparent. To the Queen, most even-tempered, least moody member of the royal family, this stern-mouthed Hanoverian heritage has been a trial since childhood.

To overcome it, she is forced to smile unremittingly every moment she is in public. If she relaxes, reporters write that "the Queen appeared displeased," which can be disastrous for the organization she is visiting. The strain of smiling for hours on end can be understood only by those who have tried to do it. The muscles of the face tremble with fatigue, the smile becomes a grimace. Elizabeth has mastered the difficulty.

Off duty, her manner is relaxed, friendly, her reactions as natural as those of any other girl. She is gentle with the nervous and the tongue-tied, for she is shy herself. She is devoted to her husband and children, and she fights continuously to keep family life separated from official duties. She infinitely prefers a small house to a palace, the country to the town, sports clothes to formal dresses. She has a lively sense of humour, and when anything amuses her, her hands go between her knees, back goes her head and she laughs unrestrainedly.

On duty, her blue eyes take on a cool expression in which can be sensed some of the spiritual loneliness imposed by the Crown. The job of being Queen calls for endless devotion to endless duties. If there is conflict between love and duty, pleasure and duty, even exhaustion and duty, there can be only one decision. It is a lot to ask of a fun-loving girl with her own family to bring up. She could not do it without her religion and an ingrained sense of dedication inherited from her father. These are the solid sources that have enabled Elizabeth to give dimension to the solemn pledge she gave the Commonwealth on her 21st birthday: "I declare before you all that my whole life, whether it be long or short, shall be devoted to your service." To this sense of dedication is now added a hard-won power of judgement. Elizabeth may lack the live-wire initiative of volatile, nimble-witted Philip, but years of unceasing work and a little heartache have brought her a level-headedness amazing in one so young.

Normally good-natured, self-disciplined, slow to anger, Elizabeth has a steel core which becomes apparent if anyone tries to tamper with her obligations as she sees them, or reflects however slightly upon the dignity of the Crown. It is well that she has this steel for, privy to secrets she may not confide even to her own husband, Elizabeth is saddled with crushing responsibilities until the day she dies.

Under the Constitution, no law is valid until it bears the ancient words "La Reyne le veult," followed by her personal signature—and Elizabeth signs nothing she has not understood. Every important Foreign Office telegram, every top-secret report must be read and filed in her memory, for while politicians come and go, the Sovereign is always there, and it is her duty to help Cabinet Ministers.

**Noblesse Oblige:** The Queen's engagements are made up a year ahead from some 2,500 requests for personal appearances—to lay foundation stones, unveil plaques, place wreaths, plant trees, visit hospitals, attend receptions, review troops, open exhibitions. The daughter of George VI is a stickler for perfection, and once she has accepted an engagement, nothing is too much trouble.

In the blinding heat of Ceylon, to please the people, she wore her heavy Coronation dress embroidered, with scores of yards of gold thread. To complete the costume, she put on a massive diamond coronet, a diamond necklace, long white gloves. Thus clad, she moved for hours through thousands of people under a burning tropical sun. Her aides were drenched with perspiration, their white uniforms sticking to their backs, but she finished the day smiling, with even her make-up unsmudged. The Governor-General murmured a compliment on her extraordinary performance. "Oh," she replied wryly, fingering the thick embroidery on her dress, "my only fear was that this gold thread would melt!"

The strain of being ever on the centre of the stage is enormous. Occasionally it is almost too great. Prince Philip watches her closely and rallies her on occasion, but sometimes even this backfires. Once, when they were approaching a large group of children, he whispered to her: "Buck up, old dear, you're drooping." The children dissolved in mirth. They were from a deaf school—lip-readers all.

Elizabeth is completely fearless, confident that no one will ever harm her. On her travels in Asia and Africa she has become locked in crowds 10,000 strong. In Nigeria an African jumped into her car—but only to present a petition. At Johannesburg's railway station a yelling old man rushed at her to ask her to go outside where his crippled son could see her (she did). In Canada a youth broke through the Mounties and asked her to give him her autograph (she did not). Blind lepers with disease-ravaged limbs crowded

about her in a leper colony, and only her compassion was affected.

***Pomp and Protocol:*** Now a new journey is in prospect. It is no secret that Palace sentiment is pro-American, wholeheartedly approving of American friends, music, entertainment, art, gadgets, cowboys. In their vigorous leadership of the Commonwealth, Elizabeth and Philip have long hankered to study the New World at first hand. Each of the 48 states, about which they are better informed than many Americans, carries some special appeal, industrial, agricultural, scenic. A career woman herself, the Queen is eager to learn more of the amazing variety of jobs held down by U.S. women, of educational and welfare programmes.

Like any other young couple, she and Philip want to add to their own home-movie collection such world-famous landmarks as Yosemite, Niagara, the Grand Canyon. They are invited to visit historic Jamestown, where British pioneers battled with the wilderness, to go to Washington, which Elizabeth glimpsed but briefly as a Princess, to spend a full day among the skyscrapers of New York and perhaps to fly to the West Coast.

Following the Queen's acceptance of the invitation, plans for The Visit slowly take shape. There are hundreds of items; each is approved or amended by the Queen personally, and the final timetable is printed for the guidance of all concerned. For the Atlantic crossing, a standard aircraft is chartered from B.O.A.C. A few changes are made to provide a private compartment for the Queen and Prince Philip; the choice of crew is left to B.O.A.C.

Now comes the selection of the Queen's party. The entourage represents the last word in teamwork. Besides being perfectionists at their own jobs, they are specialists in protocol and formal etiquette. Each has an assigned, rehearsed role. At every event there must be two ladies-in-waiting to aid the Queen. There must be two Private Secretaries and one Equerry each for the Queen and a Secretary for Prince Philip. The Press Secretary must be on hand at all times. Behind the scenes will be the Queen's first dresser, Miss "Bobo" Macdonald, and one assistant, to cope with incessant changes of clothes; a valet for Prince Philip, to produce his uniforms, with proper decorations, the instant required. All the principals must be backed up by secretaries, servants, assistants. Last and perhaps most important on a State Visit is the doctor, ready to prevent nervous and physical exhaustion, insomnia, digestive upsets, colds and headaches.

Esoteric items of information now begin ping-ponging across the Atlantic, between the entourage and their hosts in America. The Queen is strictly a three-course diner (a note which drove French chefs into melancholia during the Paris visit), prefers simple fare, is allergic to shellfish . . . "God Save the Queen" has the same tune as "My Country 'Tis of Thee" . . . British electric razors and irons will not operate on American current . . . Painting is the President's hobby . . . The Queen does not smoke, neither does Philip . . . Pocahontas was an Indian princess. (Most of this information is for the staff. Elizabeth and Philip are fond of America and know more about the country than many Americans. They require no special briefings on the United States.)

The most time-consuming item is the Queen's wardrobe. On this trip, as on all others, she will be stared at, filmed, televised and appraised front, back and sides—from the instant she shows herself in the morning until the late hour she retires at night. Every minute of every hour she must look her best, for the cameras will catch the slightest slip-up. An ordinary girl can retouch her make-up as she goes along; but the Queen of England on duty may never falter at all in her poise.

Protocol demands that every dress be new; it would be considered discourteous to appear in Canada or the United States in a dress worn in another country—or even to appear in one city in a dress worn somewhere else. Each garment must be an original design, for the Queen must never wear a model being worn by other women.

The printed schedules of The Visit to the United States and Canada show a minimum of ten days on duty, and require as many as five changes a day to allow for day and evening, rain or shine, inside and out. This means a total of 50 dresses, and because every one must be perfect the instant it is worn, each will require from three to five fittings—a total of 250 fittings superimposed.

The star numbers are the evening dresses. For these she summons Norman Hartnell, who made her Coronation dress. His job is one of extraordinary difficulty. He must bring out the distinction in the Queen's trim, if *petite*, person, her natural grace and majesty and emphasize, besides, the romantic appeal that is a concomitant of crowns. His dresses must photograph well, be light-toned to ensure her being visible against the crowds. They must harmonize with the prevailing background. As the Queen looks well in yellow, it is a safe assumption that some of her creations for The Visit will be designed to tone in with autumn foliage.

On top of all this, Hartnell must

consider the competition of hundreds of other dresses. For instance, during the State visit to Paris this spring, the Queen met the smartest women in France, each with unlimited time and money with which to procure the dress of her life. For the ultimate function, the State Banquet with the President of France, Hartnell designed a beautiful gown embroidered in pearls, topaz and gold (all costume jewellery; real gems are worn on her person, never used on her dresses) showing the fleur-de-lis and poppies of France. It was a creation that could have drowned many women; but when Elizabeth appeared on the grand staircase of the Elysée Palace, her hair blazing with diamonds, her neck circled with an emerald-and-diamond necklace, her bosom crossed with the brilliant scarlet sash of the Legion of Honour the women of Paris broke into a murmur of applause and the City asked permission to retain the dress. But it was not just the dress, or the jewels, or Elizabeth's youth; it was the extraordinary *bearing* that transformed a pretty girl into a beautiful woman, radiating an authority and grace inherited from generations of royalty.

Hartnell is also trying to please Philip, to whom, like any other woman, the Queen turns first and who, like any other husband, is capable of strange reactions. Once, viewing the sketch of a long dinner dress Philip picked up a pair of scissors, saying: "Let's hack it off at the shins." Made up to day length, the dress remains a favourite.

Daytime outfits pose special problems. For example, the Queen is continually getting out of cars before a battery of cameras, so the hems of her dresses are heavily weighted. Most girls can hold down their skirts in a wind, but not the Queen. She must hold her handbag in her left hand, often plus a bouquet—the flowers are generally damp and frequently drip down the front of her new dress—and keep the right hand free for handshaking and waving.

Every hat must have a device that keeps it clamped to the head whatever the weather. At a recent race meeting held in half a gale, the Queen was the only woman who never touched her hat, although she had to drive along the course in an open carriage.

*"The Punctuality of Kings"*: The Queen had four months to make ready for The Visit, and she needed that much time, since all the preparations had to be worked into a schedule already packed with dates made long in advance. To give an idea of how congested the Queen's time is, here is one average day's programme:

At 7 a.m., rain or shine, Bobo Macdonald wakens her mistress with a cup of tea. By 8 Elizabeth has dressed, read personal letters (envelopes from friends bear special markings) and gone through the newspapers. The last she memorizes like a professional newsman, sifting through world, Commonwealth, local news and editorials, scanning Court items and reports of yesterday's events. Then she turns on the radio for the eight o'clock news. Breakfast with Philip at 8.30 is a light one, enlivened by pungent comments on the news.

Next comes a high-spot with which nothing is allowed to interfere—part of the Queen's everlasting struggle to hold on to a normal life—a carefree get-together with the children, Charles and Anne. Then she takes time off to make her daily telephone calls to her mother and sister. (Buckingham Palace has a big switchboard with private wires and devices which enable her to speak instantly to anyone in her family and the government without operators overhearing.)

Then she hurries off to her grey-green office, where Private Secretary Sir Michael Adeane is already waiting with the day's programme and a mountain of papers. At once the two are absorbed in government reports, memoranda, general mail. As usual, the letters contain many requests, some heartbreaking, for royal help or guidance. The humblest Commonwealth citizen anywhere in the world may write directly to the Queen on any matter, knowing that his letter will be read the day it arrives and channelled to the appropriate department. While the Queen takes no direct action, letters bearing a footnote beginning: "The Queen hopes . . ." get instant results.

At 10.30 the Queen receives Major Milbank, Master of the Household —no empty title, for Buckingham Palace contains 614 rooms and requires 200 people to run it. The Queen keeps track of every detail in her own houses—the engaging and dismissing of maids, the purchase of new curtains, the household accounts, the incessant repairs. Buckingham Palace is crammed with thousands of treasures, tons of silver to clean, acres of carpets to vacuum, scores of open fireplaces to stoke and some 300 clocks to be kept wound. In this vast building the Queen and Prince Philip occupy a small suite overlooking the Palace gardens, complete with an electric-fitted kitchen for private meals. The Queen makes a daily visit to the main kitchens, a quarter of a mile from the six dining-rooms. She checks the daily menus, watches the budget (she has to pay all bills from her own pocket), works out the seating when there are guests, inspects the table minutely before they arrive.

At 11.15 comes Lord Tryon, Keeper of the Privy Purse. The Queen has mistakenly been called the world's richest woman. This sounds glamorous, but she never sees any of her income. Out of her annual grant she has to maintain huge establishments such as Buckingham Palace, St. James's Palace, Windsor Castle, Balmoral, Sandringham, whether they are publicly or privately owned, and pass them on to her successor. She must pay wages

"Next comes a high-spot with which nothing is allowed to interfere—a carefree get-together with the children, Charles and Anne."

to thousands of people, contribute to many charities, even pay for her own travel tickets. Philip has taken over much of the administration of the huge estates. By streamlining administration, putting farms on a profit-making basis (even birds shot at Balmoral are sold) and introducing labour-saving machinery, he achieves the miracle of keeping costs lower than they were 50 years ago.

It is now 11.30 a.m., and over a cup of coffee Elizabeth goes over her non-official mail with her lady-in-waiting Lady Rose Baring, who will answer it ceremoniously in longhand. Lady Rose reports to her: four dresses are ready for fitting . . . at this afternoon's function it will be Sir Charles Ponsonby's little granddaughter who will present a special bouquet featuring every national flower of the Commonwealth . . . the jewellers are troubled about a necklace setting, and what time tomorrow would be convenient for the hairdresser? . . . Coffee finished, the Queen moves back to the desk, works alone on her boxes until noon.

At 12 o'clock Elizabeth starts a series of 15-minute "audiences," granted to people in all walks of life who have some outstanding achievement to their name. If you had an appointment with her, you would be received precisely on time—"the punctuality of kings." A secretary would have briefed the Queen on your business, your family, your hobbies; and as you were shown into her study, she would come forward, smiling, to shake hands. Women first make a brief "bob," men a slight bow. You would be asked to sit in one of the comfortable armchairs. No one else would be present. There would be no interruptions, you would address her as "Ma'am"—"Your Majesty" is used only at formal functions.

It is etiquette to let the Queen lead the conversation, partly because most visitors are too nervous to do so, and partly because she does not want to be trapped into some troublesome discussion. If she asks questions, she wants plain replies—her time is too crowded for circumlocution. But her manner would be relaxed, interested, friendly. Her light, pleasant voice would charm you, you would relax, too, but you would have no impulse to presume on her informality. Her inches may be few, but her stature as The Queen is unassailable.

After about 14 minutes she would rise casually. Years of practice enable her to terminate a visit so tactfully that visitors sometimes imagine that they have done it themselves. She would shake hands unhurriedly, leave you with the impression that she was sorry to see you go. You would bow, turn, walk away, grateful that Elizabeth's visitors, unlike Queen Victoria's, are not required to back out.

At one o'clock, the Queen and Philip entertain a departing ambassador to lunch. Both are immensely interested in all he has to say and both amaze him with their knowledge of his country. By two o'clock they are in their rooms changing their clothes. Downstairs, two brown Rolls-Royces, flying the Royal Standard, creep up to the Queen's Door and ladies-in-waiting and equerries assemble.

*A Royal Visit:* Today's event is unusually important. It celebrates the reconstruction of a famous building destroyed by bombs. It is the headquarters of the Royal Empire Society (significantly proposing to change its name to Royal *Commonwealth* Society). Its rebuilding has been made possible by people of all faiths, races, creeds, colours, by gifts running from pennies to entire rooms panelled in rare Commonwealth woods. The Queen and Philip have expressed the wish to look over every inch of it, the rooms where white will sit beside black, Hindu beside Jesuit, Polynesian bishop beside Canadian miner, where neighbourliness is on a world scale.

Punctual to the minute, the Queen, dressed in blue tie-silk and off-the-face hat, followed by Philip in morning dress, goes down to the cars. As the party drives up to the building, unescorted, office windows boil with faces, pedestrians wave, men raise hats, policemen hold back the crowd. Elizabeth and Philip, beaming, walk up the spotless carpet and shake the first hands.

From here on, their progress is typical. It seems relaxed, unhurried,

but this is deceptive. Preparations for this visit have taken weeks. Palace officials have helped to rehearse each move, worked out who stands where, allotted so many minutes to each room, approved formal presentations in which bishops and High Commissioners share honours with clerks and porters. Elizabeth and Philip move smoothly from floor to floor, taking their time—the Queen will never rush through something others have taken pains to prepare. They bow, smile, pause to chat. They operate as a perfect team—the Queen ahead, rather formal, Philip a few paces behind. If the Queen gets stuck, he moves smoothly in, making jokes, asking questions, enabling her to break off and keep to the schedule.

Two hours later the Queen, still smiling and interested, gets back to the main entrance. She unveils a plaque, signs a visitors' book, shakes more hands, accepts the bouquet from the little girl (remembering her name) and, still on time, gets back into her car. Fifteen minutes later, her shoes kicked off, a cup of tea beside her, she is hard at work at her desk.

From 5 to 6.30 is another period sacred to the children's romp, supper, baths and bed-time stories. If the Queen has an early evening engagement, she dresses first to avoid cutting the children short; then she and Philip go their separate ways—he to a formal dinner of a regiment of which he is Colonel-in-Chief, she to an equally formal dinner given by a society raising money for medical research. Both will eat lightly, drink practically nothing and start for home at about 10.30, mindful that 7 a.m. the next morning will bring the start of another long day.

*An Evening Off:* Sometimes, perhaps on one evening in 20, she and Philip can dine alone, but during dinner the regular reports will come in describing that evening's debate in Parliament, and the familiar "clip-clop" may signal more boxes. If they are urgent, she deals with them. If not, she puts up her feet, arranges two cushions behind her and relaxes.

On Saturdays, if they are lucky, Philip, Elizabeth, the two children and a Scotland Yard man will pile into Philip's green Lagonda sports car and drive to Windsor Castle for the week-end—but still pursued by the boxes. At least twice a month they must take a two- or three-day trip to some Royal Borough, army regiment, air station or naval base, make speeches, shake hands.

In exchange for submission to this pitiless grip of time-schedule, there are great compensations: clothes, jewels, influence and inside knowledge of world events.

Despite recent Press criticism of the Court, the Queen is deservedly conscious of being universally loved.

Elizabeth Alexandra Mary of Windsor has had little youth—most of it was consumed in the harsh training of a Queen—but she has made herself part of the new generation just now coming of age, sharing their faith in the Commonwealth's role in world affairs. To that end, she loses no chance to promote closer ties between Commonwealth and the United States. "You are growing up in a world which is as full of possibilities of adventure as it was in the days of my predecessor, Queen Elizabeth I," she told them recently. "What the world now needs most is a solid bridge between East and West. The British Commonwealth is surely such a bridge."

Her immediate part in building the bridge is to set an example by going to the U.S., to play her part with intelligence and grace, and above all, to do her job with earnest care and forethought.

Thanks to her work behind the scenes, everything will *seem* effortless. Her plane will touch down on the Washington runway just as the President steps from his car. It will taxi up to his stand, the door will open, the guns will boom, the band will play, and Elizabeth II, smiling, fresh and assured, will walk down the gangway and shake Mr. Eisenhower's hand—on time to the minute.

---

*A*FTER installing a sprinkler system, an hotel warned its guests: "Please Do Not Smoke in Bed—You Might Drown Yourself."  —Clayton Rand

# Dress Diplomacy

## BY NORMAN HARTNELL
### *Dressmaker to H.M. Queen Elizabeth II*

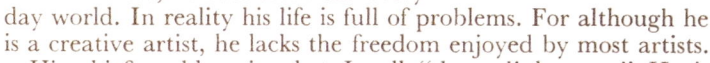

**M**OST people think of a dress designer as living in an ivory tower, remote from the everyday world. In reality his life is full of problems. For although he is a creative artist, he lacks the freedom enjoyed by most artists.

His chief problem is what I call "dress diplomacy." He is always restricted by the four "W's"—Why, When, Where, and by Whom, a design should be worn.

To overcome these he must be a psychologist, an expert on protocol, *and* a geographer! An Ambassador's wife, for example, accompanying her husband to Europe on a new appointment, needs a completely new wardrobe. The designer must be familiar with the country she is going to, know about the people and customs, in order to plan on the right lines.

And where is the busy dress designer to find time to study the world and its complex character? In my case the answer is that for years I have been reading The Reader's Digest and found it rewarding as well as enjoyable, for it has helped me to solve that question of getting around the world while staying at home. I realized it especially this summer when faced with the exciting challenge of the Royal visit to Canada and the U.S. Then it became more than ever essential that I felt familiar with the background against which I had to picture the Queen.

Through The Reader's Digest I believe I have come to know the Canadian and American peoples. I have gained an insight into their history and traditions which could not have come through any brief stay. Names engraved on the North American scene have become personalities to me. Even Pocahontas, I have learnt, took her place as "America's First Lady." The Digest has given me the essential "feel" of North America as it has of other lands nearer home.

I have had both my pleasure in reading—and my reward.

VOLUME 88

*The*
# Reader's Digest

JUNE 1966

© 1966 The Reader's Digest Association Ltd.

# PHILIP:
# Prince With a Purpose

*On his 45th birthday, the Duke of Edinburgh can look back over years in which his unorthodox ideas and determined championship of enterprise have made him an outstanding asset to the nation. In the time ahead, his qualities will be more valuable than ever before*

By Francis and Katharine Drake

During a tour of the United States last March, an important British visitor was being shown round a New York department store. His escort drew his attention to a piece of English merchandise—a tightly-rolled black umbrella, universal symbol of British respectability and regard for convention. "I wouldn't be seen dead with one of those," announced His Royal Highness Prince Philip —Duke of Edinburgh, Earl of Merioneth, Baron Greenwich, Knight of the Garter and of the Thistle.

One of the most stimulating, able, outspoken and controversial figures on the world stage today, neither resounding titles nor closeness to the throne affect Prince Philip's impact as an individual.

While a sovereign's duties have been meticulously laid down through the ages, a male consort has no constitutional function and no specified responsibilities. Traditionally he has been hemmed in by unwritten don'ts; *don't* butt into state affairs or anything controversial; *don't* try to influence the Queen; *don't* move from the background; *don't* rise above a rubber stamp. At one meeting, when a man thrust his

Ph.D. wife forward, explaining, "She's much more important than I am," Prince Philip replied kindly, "We have the same problem in our family."

It says much for Prince Philip's resourcefulness that he has managed to convert this negative status into so many positive, action-packed endeavours. He has invested the consort role with purpose, and has made himself Britain's No. 1 shot in the arm in widely separated fields.

The easy manner, the debonair appearance, convey only a fraction of the very human being who, 45 years ago this month, cropped up on a 1,000-year-old family tree. Born a Greek prince on the island of Corfu, he has no Greek blood in him but bears a royal heritage both from Queen Victoria and from King Christian IX of Denmark. From the Mountbatten side (his uncle, Earl Mountbatten, is Queen Victoria's great-grandson) come brains, looks, personality, versatility and a piledriving ambition to excel.

At Gordonstoun and later at Dartmouth Naval College, he came high in class and was a champion athlete. At 19, he was mentioned in dispatches, and later skippered one of the most efficient ships in the Mediterranean Fleet, rising to the rank of commander at the precocious age of 31.

To compensate for such rich endowment, he has the normal share of human weaknesses. He is occasionally given to "moods," and he can be short-tempered, abrupt to the point of rudeness. Brought up almost entirely among males, he is unsentimental to a degree, undemonstrative and offhand. Yet there is also an informality, a compulsive gravitation to the amusing side of things. When the Queen rested briefly in an Abbey chapel following the Coronation, Prince Philip, pointing to the Imperial State Crown on her head, whispered, "Where *did* you get that hat?"

**Out of the Red Plush.** But for some thinning on top, the Prince is little changed physically from the tall (six-foot-two), lithe Lieutenant Mountbatten of the 1947 wedding pictures, standing with chin tilted, hands clasped behind his back, a habit which continues.

At an age when most contemporaries are loosening belts, he retains a schoolboy figure and moves like the peak-conditioned athlete that he is. Only his steel-blue eyes and his mouth, prone to a tight smile when irritated, reveal that little is left of the carefree, unsophisticated midshipman who in 1939 aroused the admiration of a bashful 13-year-old named Elizabeth, daughter of King George VI.

Britain has never been more in need of some catalyst with revitalizing vision and leadership than in the years since the war. Never was there a prince more stubbornly determined to serve her purposefully. His travels to the far reaches of five continents have strengthened ties and, to lonely people in lands resigned to being overlooked, emphasized the Crown's intimate preoccupation with their welfare. Wherever he goes—Antarctica, the Khyber Pass, Katmandu, Ascension Island—his interest in human beings and their problems is unabashed, his understanding of world matters matched by few heads of state.

His most remarkable achievement, however, is that, almost single-handed, he has succeeded in detaching the Crown from the immemorial aloofness of its red-plush frame, and without sacrificing an atom of its dignity. Today it stands as the symbol of a young and vibrant force, attuned to the heartbeat of a Commonwealth numbering more than 700 million people.

**Constant Drive.** His energy is next to inexhaustible, which is fortunate considering his range of interests and nightmare number of day-by-day engagements. These are drawn up regularly on big cardboard sheets in a colour-coded mosaic. Should you ask him to dinner, should he be eager to accept, the first free date he could give you would be three months hence.

Ill or well, tired or fresh, he must keep each engagement on the dot or disappoint hundreds, sometimes thousands of people. Far from keeping down his work load, Prince Philip is constantly adding to it. If a free hour occurs on the agenda, he searches immediately for a stopgap —a quick visit to a community playground, an industrial centre, or to London's Wool Exchange to brief himself on the newest techniques. Occasionally he will let off steam in a game of polo, thundering his ponies across the field like battering rams. "It isn't his cars he drives too fast," said an observer. "It's *himself.*"

The day begins at 8 a.m., ends around midnight, and may involve hundreds of miles of travel. Should he arrive at a destination ahead of guests and welcoming committees, he buttonholes anybody handy— bricklayer, accountant, caretaker. Few are better informed than the

*Prince Philip faces his first New York press conference, March 1966*

CENTRAL PRESS

Duke of Edinburgh on what the man in the street is thinking.

When speeches are indicated, he painstakingly researches his own material, writes his own scripts, and frequently delivers them from memory. A light touch, crisp diction and that midnight-oil knowledge of his subject have made him one of the most sought-after speakers in the Commonwealth. Diehards may assail his subject-matter as "inappropriate" or "ill-advised," but in the 19 years since his marriage to the Queen, no one has accused Prince Philip of being dull.

His revitalizing force has been particularly felt in industry. Commuting from research laboratory to design centre to factory he has never stopped pressing alarm bells, exhorting management and labour to try still harder. Inspiring, cajoling, shaming, he crusades endlessly for scientific and industrial improvements, better know-how, cheaper production, modernization.

"We're certainly not a nation of nitwits," he told the National Union of Manufacturers. "Wits are our greatest national asset. We must exploit the wit of our scientists and engineers . . . of the specialist and expert . . . of the designer." Again he warned: "The 'Stop Everything' brigade is as strong as ever; it's up to you to prove that the 'Start Something' society is undismayed."

Abroad, Prince Philip has been an equally valuable asset; Lord Watkinson, chairman of the Committee for Exports to the United States, predicted that his recent American tour could lead to 100 million dollars' worth of business for Britain.

**Do - It - Yourself.** Prince Philip does more than merely *talk;* he involves himself in plans and enterprises. Among the more than 45 organizations that he heads is the Council of Industrial Design, whose Design Centre exhibitions attract over a million visitors a year. The Council's seal of approval has triggered experimental daring among young designers. The Duke keeps track of (sometimes tests personally) each uncommon item—a newfangled push-bike; fireproof textiles; hard-wearing plane luggage.

Helped by long experience and an abnormal curiosity in what makes things tick, he has developed an almost surgical approach to modern processes and problems, large and small. Sir Geoffrey De Havilland was once as much taken aback by Prince Philip's one-two-three approach to a revolutionary aircraft design as by his businessman's evaluation of its potential.

He has been known to unnerve chauffeurs by taking off his jacket and looking under the bonnet to see what is wrong with the engine. He has lent furniture movers a hand, learning the professional way of shifting loads. He is an expert pilot, with 1,500 hours' flying time to his credit. He is also a certified ship's stoker, a distinction earned when, following a belowdecks walk-out from a wartime troopship, he volunteered for coal-shovelling duty. He stuck it out, shift by sweltering shift, from Puerto Rico to Virginia.

Tens of thousands of young people look on Prince Philip as their special property. Genuinely fond of young people, he has for years infected teenagers with an awareness of approaching responsibility.

His Duke of Edinburgh's Award Scheme, for boys and girls aged 14–20, encourages public service, hobbies, fitness and expeditions. Self-reliance is the keynote. Some 130,000 young people from Britain and the Commonwealth have won awards; he personally presents the special Gold Award at Buckingham Palace.

As president of the National Playing Fields Association, Prince Philip has set as his goal playgrounds not more than 500 yards apart in built-up areas, six acres or more of recreational space for every 1,000 inhabitants.

His fund-raising campaigns have succeeded in increasing elbow-room to the extent of 2,124 football fields, 1,700 cricket grounds, 2,058 tennis courts, plus innumerable gyms, pavilions, and parks. His promise to "go anywhere to open a new playground" has been kept.

The worldwide despoiling of animal wildlife provoked Prince Philip into accepting the British presidency of the World Wildlife Fund. An ardent bird watcher, the Duke has gone so far as to make cats *non grata* at Buckingham Palace.

**Polished Performance.** The activity in which the public usually visualizes royalty is the formal occasion—an endless round of banquets, tree plantings, cornerstone layings, openings of charitable institutions, agricultural and industrial shows, presentations of honours and awards. These appearances are all-important because they demonstrate the Crown's unwavering interest in national life.

Most thrilling are the red-carpet functions attended by heads of state, diplomats, top military brass. Whether Prince Philip participates simply as the Queen's escort (as at the State Opening of Parliament) or alone as her official representative abroad, the form is equally rigid. It calls for a sartorially resplendent Prince in full-dress uniform, gleaming with decorations. His bearing, grace and elegance reflect the pride and dignity of Britain.

Oddly enough, the informal Prince adapts well to these regimented occasions. Like the Queen, he carefully observes protocol, as well as the code of politeness which prescribes that a consort must always stand a pace or two behind the Sovereign.

Alone or together, the royal pair take immense pride in giving a polished performance. Mistakes are rare—none since that distant day when the Duke appeared in the wrong uniform for a parade. Even as he chats affably with a welcoming committee, Prince Philip's quarter-deck eye will be noting the layout. It will be his toe that nudges back a chair informally lined up with the Queen's. He checks if microphones are too high, lights too blinding, photographers too close. Always a step or two behind, telepathically aware of the Queen's requirements, he may point out some feature that she missed, adroitly disengage her from a bore, detain the reception line with some gay pleasantry if she is crowded. His unobtrusive support is so constant that an elderly courtier, veteran of five reigns, recently remarked, "Can't think how we ever got along without him."

**Family Man.** The law that an Englishman's home is his castle applies mainly to those not inhabiting castles. The public has a ravenous interest in the Royal Family's home life, and Prince Philip fights to reserve this area. Reporters gather backstairs gossip from *vendeuses* (who reveal that Prince Andrew tried on his mother's hats during a fitting), from footmen (who collided with royal tricycles in sacrosanct state apartments), from tradesmen in pubs.

The family circle, a lively, well-adjusted one, means much to Prince Philip, who as a boy was shunted from relative to relative. He takes pride in his children and lets nothing interfere with the time set aside daily for their companionship. He delights in teaching them to ride, groom their own horses, swim, sail, box, birdwatch.

Both parents are old-fashioned disciplinarians. Spankings, though rare, have followed out-of-line behaviour; politeness and obedience are required at all times. Family decisions are arrived at jointly, such as the precedent-shattering one to let the children experience the give-and-take of boarding schools, even one as far away as Australia.

Thirty years ago, Prince Philip's headmaster, bringing him to the attention of the Admiralty as a "born leader," wrote: "Prince Philip will need the exacting demands of a great Service to do justice to himself. His best is outstanding; his second best is not good enough."

The service the headmaster had in mind was the Royal Navy. The one to which Prince Philip was eventually called has proved considerably more exacting. But, to his credit, not once has it been noted that he has settled for second best. His over-all performance must indeed be called "outstanding."

---

## Local Colour

*R*ENTAVILLA, the firm which rents houses on the French Riviera and in other Mediterranean areas, operates an artificial sun-tanning booth in London for clients who don't want to look conspicuously pale when they arrive at their holiday destinations.  —UPI

*Prince Charles arriving at Trinity College, Cambridge*

VOLUME 94

# *The* Reader's Digest

JUNE 1969

© 1969 The Reader's Digest Association Ltd.

# THE NEW PRINCE OF WALES

*People are finding that the
young man destined to be
king is a surprisingly "decent,
ordinary sort of chap"*

### BY PETER BROWNE

WHEN Prince Charles is invested as Prince of Wales and presented to his people at Caernarvon Castle next month, an audience of 500 million will look on. For this colourful scene will be a worldwide television spectacular, unequalled for pageantry since the coronation of his mother Queen Elizabeth II.

For Charles, however, his investiture as the twenty-first Prince of Wales will be a double ordeal. There is the natural tension: the Duke of Windsor, at his own installation in 1911 when only 17, was "half-fainting with heat and nervousness." Further, Charles is well aware of threats by Welsh extremists to sabotage the 1969 ceremony. (In Cardiff last June, they greeted him with jeers and exploding smoke bombs.)

Demonstrators will probably parade with banners proclaiming "No Foreign Prince" and "Remember Llywelyn"—referring to Llywelyn ap Gruffydd, last *Welsh* Prince of

Wales, who fell in battle against Edward I in 1282. In fact, as Charles explained in a recent broadcast, "I'm descended three times over from the original Welsh princes. My grandmother, Queen Elizabeth, is descended twice over through both sides, so I seem to have quite a lot of Welsh blood in me."

But the great majority of Welshmen plan to offer the Prince such a welcome that, says Caradog Prichard, Bard of Wales, "to call this the Land of Song will be a typical Saxon understatement."

**Royal Modesty.** Despite his imposing roll call of titles—Duke of Cornwall, Duke of Rothesay, Earl of Carrick and Baron of Renfrew, Lord of the Isles and Great Steward of Scotland—the 20-year-old young man who will be swearing his allegiance to the Queen, his mother, is without trace of self-importance. Signing cheques or documents, Charles simply uses his Christian name, never bothering to add "P" for *Princeps*. At last year's Royal Film Performance, he looked at the row of medals worn by a film company executive, then indicated his own single decoration, a Coronation Medal, with a rueful "I'm doing rather badly, I'm afraid."

The first Prince of Wales to enjoy a full university career, Charles has a reputation at Cambridge for hard work—and in this he is like his namesake, the first King Charles, who as Prince of Wales was "addicted to grave studies." Determined

to succeed on his own merits, Charles passed his first exams in archaeology and anthropology only a few marks short of the top possible result. "He soaks up information like a sponge," says a former schoolmaster.

Unlike his great-uncle Prince Edward, who at Oxford in 1912 drove a Daimler, Charles's usual transport at Cambridge is an old bicycle. He seems incapable either of being flamboyant or of taking himself over-seriously. Heads seldom turn as he walks by with his loping stride, a lean five feet eleven inches tall, and wearing tweed jacket and rumpled corduroys. Nothing marks out the heir to the throne except perhaps the flop of hair over his forehead. (A school friend once asked him about his "Beatle" hair style. "You mean the Beatles have Prince Charles haircuts," he retorted. "This was my style long before they were heard of!")

Like any other undergraduate, Charles cooks his own breakfast, and queues for a 5s. 6d. dinner in Hall beneath the portrait of his ancestor, Henry VIII, who founded the college in 1546. He carries a National Union of Students card, shops at "Marks and Sparks," takes an active part in the college dramatic society, contributes to the student newspaper, *Varsity*.

Music is his passion, as it was for several of his predecessors. As a boy George IV played the cello, and

so does Charles—though in his hands, he says wryly, the instrument sounds like a squeaking church door.

The future King Charles III is very much of his generation. He is clothes-conscious: "When it comes to matters of detail, like pockets or seaming," comments his tailor, "he knows exactly what he wants." He enjoys a party—walking across the college lawns to his first May Ball, he heard a steel band playing in the distance, and promptly swept his partner into an exuberant cha-cha. Says his Cambridge tutor, "The whole point about Prince Charles is that he's a thoroughly normal undergraduate."

**Born to be King.** But unlike his friends, Charles has a fixed destiny —one of which, since birth, he has been constantly made aware.

When Victoria gave birth to her first son, Bertie, the Minister who congratulated her on "a very fine boy" was sharply reproved: "A very fine *Prince, Sir James*." The same distinction was scrupulously observed on the night of November 14, 1948.

As several thousand Londoners milled expectantly outside Buckingham Palace, a handwritten bulletin fixed to the Palace railings announced that "The Princess Elizabeth was safely delivered of a Prince." A 41-gun salute was fired from the Tower of London. Cascading water in the Trafalgar Square fountains was floodlit blue for a boy. Bellringers at Westminster Abbey welcomed their future king with a peal of 5,040 changes.

From the beginning his parents were determined to give Charles as ordinary an upbringing as possible. Thus, after Princess Elizabeth came to the throne in 1952, the rattle of roller skates was heard in Buckingham Palace, as Charles explored the 15 miles of corridors and 600 rooms.

There were certain royal disciplines, however, that could not be discarded. Charles and his sister Anne had to learn to stand still for long periods, as necessary rehearsal for public ceremonies to come. Neither of the children was allowed to take advantage of being Royalty. When Charles walked into a room leaving the door open, his father stopped a footman from closing it. "He's got hands," said Philip. "Let him do it himself." While a Sandringham policeman, helmet knocked askew, was pondering the proper procedure for an officer snowballed by the heir to the throne, Philip called out, "Don't just stand there —throw some back!"

Like any heir to the throne, Charles was taught, as had been Edward the Black Prince some 600 years before, to "sitte at mete seemly," and to "danse and synge." There were classroom lessons at the Palace from his governess, Miss Peebles. But in November 1956, at the age of eight, Charles was registered at Hill House, Knightsbridge

—the first heir to the throne to attend an ordinary school.

At Hill House it became evident that there were gaps even in Charles's carefully "normal" upbringing. He had never been in a shop nor handled money, for example. So it was necessary to teach him the value of the coins on which his mother's head was stamped.

His parents were well satisfied when he left Hill House after nine months with a report describing him as "a good average schoolboy." Yet when he went on to boarding school at Cheam, in Berkshire, the other boys found it difficult to regard him as average, and cautiously kept their distance. Charles was miserably lonely at first.

He was treated as just another boy —sleeping on the same kind of unsprung bed in the same bare, unheated dormitory as anyone else, cleaning his shoes, waiting at table. But he had some problems peculiarly his own. About to write his first letter home, he sought advice: "I know my mother is the Queen—but how do I put that on the envelope?" Another time, after a stomach upset, he confessed that he was unused to such rich food.

Eventually he was accepted by the

*The arms which Prince Charles will be entitled to bear after his investiture*

schoolboys of Cheam. The verdict on him in his second term was, "a decent, ordinary sort of chap"— which, in twentieth century terms, is a high accolade.

For Charles, the freedom of holiday time was doubly enjoyable. There was the fun of driving a go-kart at Sandringham—even if, after he skidded into a rose bush, the engine was tuned down to 12 m.p.h. At Balmoral there were fishing and camping expeditions with his father, then table tennis in the staff pantry with butlers and footmen. But on any venture outside the royal estates there was the risk of being recognized. It was difficult even to try to buy ice-cream in a Norfolk village on a Sunday without someone making a fuss. "Where is the example?" thundered the Lord's Day Observance Society. "In which direction are the children being led?"

All hope of avoiding the limelight vanished in July 1958. Watching television in his headmaster's study, Charles saw 36,000 Welshmen gathered for the Commonwealth Games at Cardiff Arms Park burst into a storm of cheering as his mother's voice announced that he had been created Prince of Wales.

Charles was destined to attend

his father's old school, Gordonstoun —celebrated for two cold showers a day, long runs before breakfast, and mountaineering expeditions. To the 13-year-old boy it sounded "pretty gruesome."

As at Cheam, he was expected to prove himself. His most frequent chore during his first term was shifting dustbins. On the rugby field, he got his share of rough handling, including a broken nose. But one of his characteristics is a quiet determination to make a success of whatever has to be done. "I think he's pretty good," decided one classmate. "I mean, he's not stuck up like some people here with far less to be stuck up about."

It became accepted that Charles was something of a "loner." Unenthusiastic about organized games, he preferred to spend his spare time working in the pottery shop or indulging his growing interest in music. "I wish he was a bit better on the trumpet," complained one boy. "I know he likes it, but he drives me mad."

**Easy Manner.** Those who knew him were never overawed. A girl who danced with him at a local party described him as "a super dancer. He knows all the latest wiggles." At a garden party for 600 students at the Palace of Holyroodhouse, the Queen's official residence in Scotland—to which he was summoned from Gordonstoun—some of those present failed even to recognize him. When a pretty girl walked past without shaking hands, the 17-year-old prince decided it was time to exercise his royal prerogative. "Hi!" he called after her. "Wait a minute!"

Early in 1966, Charles was on his way to Australia for the next stage of his education—at Timbertop, a hutted community in the outback where boys of Melbourne's Geelong Grammar School spend a year fending for themselves. The only domestic staff is a cook; responsible for their own studies, the boys also do all the chores, from tending pigs to chopping wood.

**Outdoor Life.** Here, Charles was happier than he had ever been. Far from the goldfish-bowl existence at home, he responded to the easygoing friendliness of Australians. The life was strenuous, but there was also time to fish, and form a trumpet trio; to try gold-panning and sheep-shearing. "I made rather a mess of it," he admits, "and left a somewhat shredded sheep."

Markedly more poised and self-confident, Charles returned to finish at Gordonstoun. During his final year there he was appointed head boy. And in October 1967 he entered Trinity College.

Having begun the task of learning Welsh a year ago, Charles is continuing it now during the April-June term at the University College of Wales in Aberystwyth. Future historians may well rank him the most conscientious of all the Princes of Wales. Many of his predecessors never even visited their principality: most were invested either at London or Windsor.

At the investiture, on July 1, the Queen will place on Charles's head a coronet as token of principality, into his hand the golden rod of government, and on his third finger the ring of responsibility. And the prince will swear to her the traditional oath. "I Charles, Prince of Wales, do become your liege man of life and limb and of earthly worship, and faith and truth I will bear unto you to live and die against all manner of folks."

The day promises spectacle enough to attract an estimated 250,000 visitors to Caernarvon. Windows overlooking the castle square have been rented at sky-high prices. Souvenirs range from Welsh Dragon banners to Wedgwood mugs stamped with pictures of the castle. The Ministry of Public Building and Works is selling the 4,000 chairs to be used by invited guests for £12 each.

**"Ich Dien."** What of the future? Charles will return to Cambridge in the autumn to complete his degree course. His twenty-first birthday, in November, will make no difference to his life as an undergraduate, although as Duke of Cornwall he becomes entitled to the full revenues of the Duchy—approaching £200,000 a year.*

And after he takes his degree? Since Charles's father has demolished the artificial barriers that long prevented a member of the royal family from taking an active hand in public affairs, Charles will have greater opportunity than any previous Prince of Wales. Suggestions have ranged from a colonial governorship to full-time management of a major charity. A poll of Welshmen showed that three out of four would like him to act as unofficial ambassador for Wales, as the Duke of Edinburgh does for all Britain.

Whichever direction Charles's career takes, it will be influenced by a strong social conscience. To him, the royal motto, "Ich Dien"—"I Serve"—is no empty phrase. Those who know this quiet prince best believe that he will fulfil a tutor's advice given in 1637 to that other Prince, who became Charles II: "Win people's hearts, and then you will have all they have; you cannot have more."

* As the twenty-fourth Duke since 1337, Charles is landlord of 140,000 acres spreading far beyond the Cornish boundary. Much of Dartmoor is his, with tracts of Dorset, Gloucestershire, Wiltshire, Somerset, and some valuable land in London, including the Oval of Test Match fame.

---

Puzzled by the woman driver's excuse that she was making an "S" turn, the policeman asked her to explain.

"You start by making a 'U' turn," she said, "then you realize you are in a one-way street."  —B. J. Kallaway, Cheadle, Cheshire

VOLUME 103

# *The* Reader's Digest

AUGUST 1973

© 1973 The Reader's Digest Association Ltd.

# Once Upon a Royal Visit

### By Robert Collins

## A prairie man recalls another, simpler time when royalty came to Canada

IN MOST respects that spring of 1939 in Central Canada was like any other prairie spring: a tantalizing mixture of hope and despair. The redwing blackbirds sang cheerfully, but May came in hot and dry. Grasshopper eggs hatched in the sun, threatening another plague that would strip the fields of every living thing. The horse-killing disease, encephalomyelitis, was making the rounds again.

Then one morning the news raced along the telephone party-line to our Saskatchewan farm: *"The King and Queen are coming to Canada!"* A shock wave of pure delight ran behind it. Never before had a reigning British monarch set foot on Canadian soil.

To most of us in those simpler times, kings and queens were holy figures, and none more than George VI and Queen Elizabeth. The timing was perfect. The world was on the brink of war. Canada was staggering into its tenth year of depression. Now, out of a fairy tale, Their Gracious Majesties were coming to lighten our dreary days. Nowhere was George VI more revered than in our house, six miles south of the village of Shamrock.

My father was a patriot. Born in Belfast, raised in England, almost killed by poison gas in the First

World War, he was as loyal a subject as the Empire ever had. When the National Anthem played he stood to attention, and expected everyone else to do the same. Once in the Shamrock community hall, during *God Save the King,* I saw him silence a gaggle of sniggering teenagers with a glance. Years later when we had a radio, the Anthem caught us at bedtime. Instantly Dad sprang to his feet, ramrod straight, in his combinations.

**Impossible Dream.** So we rejoiced in the Royal Visit news, even though we would never see Their Gracious Majesties. They would cross Canada by train but their nearest stop, on May 25, would be Moose Jaw, 60 miles away. The return fare for our family was about ten dollars—food and clothing for a month during the Depression. Moose Jaw might as well have been the moon.

We could not afford a battery-operated radio, but the Regina *Leader-Post,* arriving by train, was our lifeline to the world. George VI, the *Leader* said, was packing most of his 50 uniforms for the long journey. Small communities across Canada were planting trees and scrubbing down city halls for the occasion. The local Imperial Order,

ROBERT COLLINS, a frequent contributor to US and Canadian magazines, is a former editor of *Toronto Life* magazine and has written some 20 articles for *Reader's Digest.* He has also published five books. Though Saskatchewan born and bred, he has lived in Eastern Canada since 1948.

Daughters of the Empire, was sponsoring an essay contest: "Why I Wish to be in Moose Jaw on May 25." An entire Ottawa school was getting long breaks so the children could line the street, wave flags and cheer, to help the nervous horses of the Royal Canadian Dragoons get used to crowds.

My father wistfully studied the *Leader-Post.* Our sole cash income was his wartime disability pension, about 15 dollars a month. With it he stayed out of serious debt (a point of honour with him), and eked out a living for all the animals and humans on our farm. Still, 15 dollars *would* just about cover the trip to Moose Jaw . . .

On Saturday, May 6, the King and Queen boarded the *Empress of Australia* for Canada. On Sunday, the year's first dust storm swirled across the fields. It was mild compared to the one that struck the next day. For almost two days a 40-mile-an-hour wind lifted the topsoil and blacked out southern Saskatchewan. Sand seeped round doors, under windowsills. Lamps were lit at noon. Cars stopped, with visibility down to zero, and on the near-by Canadian Pacific Railway mainline, a train had to wait for the air to clear. The little wheat plants clung stubbornly to the fields, but we knew the next storm might wipe out them—and our hopes—for another year. And my father knew he'd need that 15 dollars.

Now the Royal Visit news

crowded everything off the front pages. The *Leader-Post* instructed readers to address the King as "Sir" and the Queen as "Ma'am," should we happen to meet them. Fat chance! We read that grandstand seats in Toronto were selling for five dollars each, and silently hated Toronto a little more.

On the morning of May 17, the *Empress of Australia* docked at Quebec City, in sight of the Plains of Abraham. "THUNDERING CHEERS ECHO ALONG CLIFFS" screamed the *Leader-Post*. My father was in Shamrock that day, and came home with a grim look of a man about to slay a dragon. "Mother," he said. "The boys *have* to see this. We're *going,* come hell or high water!"

I can only guess at how they must have weighed and worried that enormous decision. "How can we leave the baby chicks? They're only two weeks old!" said Mother. "And the cows have to be milked at night. No, you three go. I'll stay and look after the place."

"The chickens will be all right," Dad said firmly. "The cows can wait till morning. We're all going." And it was settled.

If I had ever doubted the power of the King, not any more. I was 14, but I had never been to Moose Jaw, nor ridden on a train. We never left the cows unmilked. And those 250 chicks were a vital part of our 1939 food and income strategy.

But we were going! And now we dared to wallow with the rest of Canada in a royalty-worshipping binge. The blue, silver and gold 12-coach royal train sped west through waves of adulation: "MONTREALERS CRAM THE STREETS," "A MILLION

TORONTONIANS CHEER THEM." From Ottawa, the *Leader-Post* revealed that the King had "a real man's voice, warm and cordial . . . His tanned skin, clear eyes and strong handgrip tell a story of health and clean living." And the Queen? "The camera misses her inner light . . . quite like someone out of a fairy tale . . . you expect her to dissolve in thin air at any moment . . ."

At the week-end, God threw in a bonus—two inches of glorious, life-giving rain; more came early in the week. Thursday, May 25, dawned clear and muddy. We rose early and gave the animals enough food for 24 hours. The dirt roads were a quagmire but we hitched up a team and wagon and drove to Shamrock, the wheels flinging showers of mud around us.

**Whistle Stop.** The 10 a.m. train chuffed in, late as usual and half-full of patriots from all along the line. The coach smelled deliciously of age and cinders. The whistle sent a great full-bellied wail echoing off the grain elevators, and the train lunged forward. We were off to Moose Jaw to see the King!

Mother had packed a huge basket of food to see us through lunch and supper. But the excitement and the hunger were contagious. Everyone else was eating and we ate too, demolishing every crumb.

We reached Moose Jaw in mid-afternoon. Was there any city so big, so magnificent? Some of the buildings were four, maybe five storeys high! Its population of 20,000 had only doubled that day, but I'm sure I counted half a million people. Outside the railway station a squad of Mounties manoeuvred in full dress uniform. For ten years I had read *King of the Royal Mounted;* I knew *Sergeant Silk the Prairie Scout* by heart; but I had never seen a Mountie in scarlet. If the squad had trampled me on the spot, I would have died with a smile.

We passed a little platform where local dignitaries would meet Their Gracious Majesties at about 9.30 that night. Then we let the crowds sweep us along Main Street. Then, as now, it ran arrow-straight from the station through the heart of Moose Jaw. All the action was here —Union Jacks, Red Ensigns, and multi-coloured bunting fluttered from every lamp post; an enormous electric organ stood on the pavement to entertain the crowds and serenade the royal visitors.

At five o'clock wooden barricades were already going up to shield shop windows from the billowing crowds. Dad found us places near the kerb, then marched away with a thousand other veterans to get an armband and beret, line the parade route and form a guard of honour for his King.

All through that long, long evening it rained sporadically, and our Sunday finery sagged. Moose Jaw did its best to entertain us. The organ played, Mounties pranced on matching bay horses, Girl Guides and Scouts trooped by, Moose Jaw's schoolchildren paraded and then—horrors!—hundreds of them took up positions in front of us. And it was nearly 9.30!

Then a kind schoolteacher looked back, saw us and beckoned. "Go! Hurry!" cried my mother. We boys squeezed in among the schoolchildren.

"The Royal Train has arrived," boomed a loudspeaker. Somewhere on that platform the local aldermen and wives were having their moment with royalty. Finally the screams: "THEY'RE COMING!" The din turned into one long hoarse roar. Leaning far out, I glimpsed my father, standing so straight I feared he would never bend again.

The motorcade came, but moving too fast, for the aldermen had taken up too much time. I glimpsed a dark, smiling woman and a serious man in a peaked, military cap. Behind in a second car, as consolation prize, was Prime Minister Mackenzie King. In a flash they were gone.

The King and Queen drove eight blocks up Main Street that night and hurried back to their train to keep to their timetable. Their allotted time in Moose Jaw was exactly 30 minutes. My mother never saw their faces, although she said the Queen had a lovely hat.

We elbowed our way towards the station, dazed with fatigue and excitement. Moose Jaw set off fireworks, prepared Main Street for an open-air dance, and opened a fair. But each side-show was five cents, which we couldn't afford. Anyway, it was time to go home. At one o'clock in the morning, the train crept slowly into the country. We boys stayed up all night, prowling the aisles, drinking the water cooler dry and unwinding from the miracle of the day.

At dawn we reached Shamrock, hitched up our horses, and drove home through the dew, the clean aroma of wet earth and the blessed prairie silence. A huge red sun climbed in the east. Our waiting animals eyed us reproachfully. We fed them, filled ourselves with bacon and eggs, and tumbled into bed. We did not feel cheated that we had seen so little. We had seen so *much*.

For father was right when he scrimped and sacrificed to shepherd us to Moose Jaw that day in 1939. It was one of those moments when logical is illogical. He gave us a glimpse not just of a king but of the world. It was 15 dollars well spent.

---

## Labour Exchange

A JOB applicant listed "Turnover" on an employment form as his reason for leaving a job.

"What do you mean by turnover?" asked the interviewer.

"They turned my job over to somebody else," the applicant explained.

—George Dolan in Fort Worth *Star-Telegram*

VOLUME 107

## *The* Reader's Digest

AUGUST 1975

© 1975 The Reader's Digest Association Ltd.

# THE QUEEN MOTHER
## Her Glorious Years

### By Peter Browne

Radiant at 75, she enchants countless Britons with
a rare candour and irrepressible sense of fun

CAREFULLY timed, the programme of the royal visit to Leeds allowed for no more than a brief word in the Town Hall with the men who had formed the naval guard of honour. But Queen Elizabeth the Queen Mother, who cares more for people than protocol, stopped to chat to a leading seaman from the aircraft carrier *Ark Royal* —only to find that a cold had robbed him of his voice.

A look of concern crossed her face, and while a dither of dignitaries furtively consulted their watches she rummaged in her handbag, triumphantly producing a throat lozenge. The sailor gratefully popped it into his mouth; and no one who knows the Queen Mother would doubt those who claim to have seen a royal wink before she went smiling on her way.

Wherever she goes, formality melts under the warmth of a personality as homely as the battered tea cosy she takes on her travels. Characteristically, while walking through a children's home she spotted a little girl solemnly bathing a doll, and bent to whisper: "Don't forget to wash behind her ears." Dancing with a nervous and fumble-footed student at a university ball, she encouraged him: "Cheer up, you're doing fine. You haven't knocked my tiara off—yet!"

Royal portrait painter Pietro Annigoni once said: "It is hard to imagine a kinder, warmer, more appealing human being"—an opinion shared unanimously by a nation which has coined its own affectionate title for her. As a heckler at Speaker's Corner in Hyde Park shouted at an anarchist orator demanding the overthrow of the monarchy: "What about the Queen Mum?"

Sheepishly the anarchist acknowledged his blunder. "Well, she's different."

**Not by the Book.** Theoretically a pensioner (this month marks her seventy-fifth birthday) she should by all the accepted rules of age be taking life easy. But the Queen Mother blithely makes her own rules and thrives on new experience. She looked forward eagerly to flying by Concorde to visit the Shah of Iran last April, and was much disappointed when a technical hitch ruled out that adventure. After all, 23 years ago she was the first member of the royal family to handle the controls of a jet airliner—gleefully radioing to the RAF squadron of which she was Honorary Air Commodore: "Thoughts turned to 600 Squadron. What the passengers thought, I really would not like to say!"

In 1974 the Queen Mother's diary listed 152 public engagements at home, plus a six-day tour of Canada. She is perpetually in demand. Nor will she brook any suggestions that possibly she might ease up on the more arduous functions—like this year's Albert Hall ceremonies when some 4,000 graduates of London University filed past to be presented individually, or the long Hyde Park review of Territorial units on a chilling April day.

Her sense of duty is unshakeable and her activities would exhaust anyone half her age. Her own schedule is formidable enough, but when her daughter the Queen is overseas she takes on many extra duties—acting as counsellor of State, receiving ambassadors, holding investitures. Then there are more than 300 public bodies at home and abroad of which she is patron: they range from The Nuffield Foundation to the Keep Britain Tidy Group, Dr. Barnardo's to the Royal Academy of Dramatic Art. Young in heart, she shows immense enthusiasm for her role as Chancellor of London University. As one student puts it: "She's great fun. Everyone gets on like a bomb with her."

No one has opened more hospital wards, planted more trees, presented more regimental colours — yet she makes each occasion seem fresh and interesting. "She lays a foundation stone," marvels one observer, "as though she has just discovered a new and delightful way of spending an afternoon."

When the royal Rolls glides up and the dazzling figure of the Queen Mother emerges dressed in pastel pink or blue, the first impression is of an almost theatrical splash of colour, the second of a smile so infectious that it is impossible not to respond. The direct blue eyes beneath the feathered hat sparkle with

PHOTOGRAPH: FOX PHOTOS. ILLUSTRATIONS: GARY KEANE, BASED ON PHOTOGRAPHS IN "ELIZABETH OF GLAMIS" BY DAVID DUFF (FREDERICK MULLER LTD.)

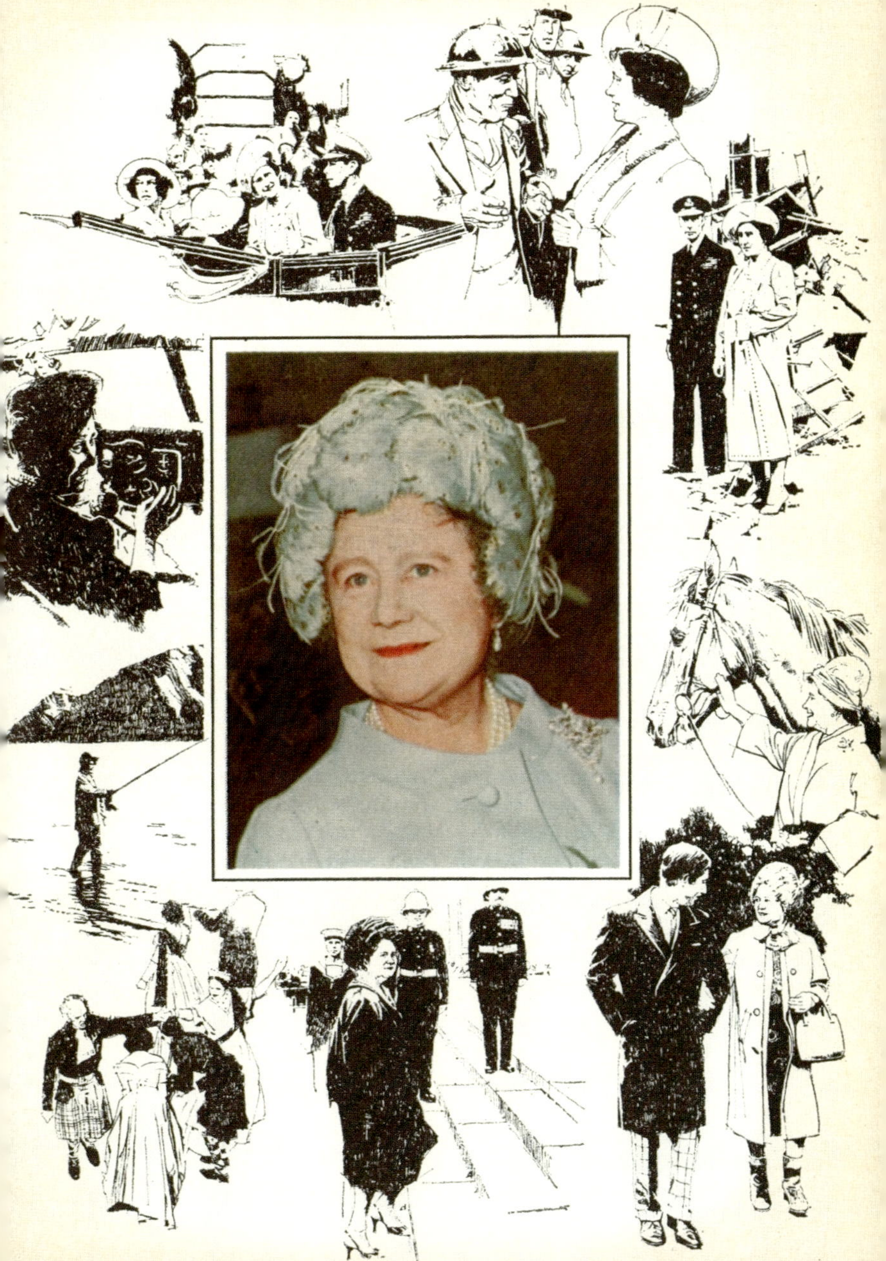

zest; her voice is light and clear, and she has a habit of tilting her head to one side while listening so that those she meets feel they have never before been so witty and interesting. Even the shyest find themselves chatting easily to her.

Completely unselfconscious, she has a rare candour, particularly about herself. The proofs of a birthday photograph he had taken were returned to Cecil Beaton with a message from her private secretary: "Her Majesty feels that since she has battled her way through a number of years she could not have come through completely unscathed. Would it be possible at this stage to take away the retouching?"

Press photographers hold her in high regard, for she can always be counted on to know the moment, the background and the lighting that will provide just the picture they want. On one occasion a minor bureaucrat brusquely tried to push a Fleet Street cameraman out of her path. "Please don't do that," she said, an unaccustomed edge to her voice. "We are old friends."

**Royal Prerogative.** Nothing upsets the Queen Mother more than interference from what she terms "officialdom." Refusing to be hurried through a visit, she insists that it matters much more not to miss anyone than to be a few minutes late. "Queen Elizabeth has a capacity for spotting the most humble-looking individual at any gathering," comments her private secretary, Sir Martin Gilliat, "and making that person feel the very one she most wants to talk to."

Among the millions who know her only from newspaper photographs are many who instinctively sense her warmheartedness, and appeal to her for advice. She sees every letter, checks every answer, and has a knack of finding human solutions to problems that escape the impersonal net of the welfare state. Years of experience have given her an expert knowledge of the organizations best able to help; often she will quietly follow up a case, particularly if it involves the breakdown of a family, although few of those who benefit ever know that the Queen Mother has taken a personal interest in them.

Correspondence apart, she spends many hours at her desk. In advance of every visit there is a pile of papers to be digested: background information on the place concerned, reminders of the people she has already met and notes on those she will meet for the first time. When she has to hold an investiture for the Queen, she demands a briefing on each of the several hundred recipients—and talks to every single one, leaving them astonished at her close knowledge of their work.

Born Lady Elizabeth Bowes-Lyon on August 4, 1900, the Queen Mother was the youngest but one of the ten children of the Earl and Countess of Strathmore. Her childhood was divided between her parents' Hertfordshire house, St. Paul's Walden Bury, and the medieval castle of Glamis, in Angus, which has belonged to the Lyon family for over 600 years.

For Elizabeth, Glamis meant family holidays north of the border each autumn, but "home" was the picturesque Queen Anne house in Hertfordshire where she grew up as one of a close-knit, happily boisterous group, and was educated first by her mother, later by governesses. (Years afterwards she found a copy book in which she had pencilled a terse essay: "Some governesses are nice, and some *are not.*")

**Salad Days.** She was 14 when the First World War broke out, and the family turned Glamis Castle into a convalescent hospital. An army sergeant who spent six months there remembered "the loveliest pair of blue eyes I'd ever seen—eloquent eyes that could speak for themselves." Her arrival in London after the war was described by the Countess of Airlie: "Lady Elizabeth was very unlike the cocktail-drinking, chain-smoking girls who came to be regarded as typical of the 'twenties. Her radiant vitality and a blending of gaiety, kindness and sincerity made her irresistible to men."

Among them was the Duke of York, King George V's second son, a friend of the Bowes-Lyon brothers. The Duke, who was extremely shy and suffered from a stammer, met Elizabeth at a dance in 1920, when he was 24 and she five years younger.

The following year, staying at Glamis, he wrote to his mother, Queen Mary: "The more I see of her, the more I like her." Soon he was deeply in love. Said the King: "You'll be a lucky fellow if she accepts you."

But Elizabeth knew that joining the royal family would mean exchanging independence and privacy for a lifetime of public scrutiny. It was two years before the Duke's persistence won her over. In April 1923, they were wed in Westminster Abbey and later made their London home at 145 Piccadilly.

Before marriage, the Duke of York had been moody and introspective; now friends saw in him a new sureness and vigour. With his wife at his side to help him through the ordeal which public speaking entails for anyone afflicted with a stammer, he absorbed himself in the problems of industrial relations, taking on a role comparable to that of the Duke of Edinburgh today.

**Change of Order.** For 13 years they lived contentedly in the royal circle, with duties to perform but time to enjoy raising their two daughters. There seemed no reason why their pleasant life should not continue, even after the death of King George V in January 1936. It was the Duke of York's elder brother, the Prince of Wales, who became King and, once he married, his own children would be next in line of succession. But December that year brought the abdication crisis. The uncrowned Edward VIII left England to marry Mrs Simpson and become Duke of Windsor—and a quiet couple who had never sought the limelight suddenly found themselves King George VI and Queen Elizabeth.

The King came to the throne on a surge of goodwill, for the nation felt that fate had dealt with him unkindly. Later, the Archbishop of Canterbury was to write to him: "I find everywhere the same testimony to the impression which Your Majesty and the Queen have made upon your people during the first year of your reign. At first, the feeling was one of sympathy and hope. It has now become a feeling of admiration and confidence."

In the quarter century of King George V's reign, the popular idea of a queen consort had been moulded by the awesomely regal Queen Mary. Now the warmth and friendliness of Queen Elizabeth transformed that image. In France in 1938 on her first state visit abroad with her husband, her all-white wardrobe was a fashion sensation. At a Washington reception a year later an enthusiastic Senator congratulated the King, "My, you're a great Queen picker!"

The easy informality of their welcome in North America strengthened George VI's long-held conviction that the monarchy needed the common touch it had never known under his father. In his wife he had the perfect ally, and the coming of

war in 1939 hastened the shaping of a new bond between Crown and people.

When the blitz on London began the King and Queen remained at Buckingham Palace, although it was obviously a target for German bombers, and was hit twice during the first few days—once so accurately that the royal couple, upstairs in a sitting-room, saw the bombs slant past the window to explode only 80 yards away. "I'm glad we've been bombed," said the Queen. "It makes me feel I can look the East End in the face."

**Tour de Force.** With the King she would visit districts bombed overnight, picking her way through still-smoking rubble to comfort shocked survivors. "Although her heart was breaking," one of her staff has recalled, "she could turn to a woman who had lost everything and find something kind and loving to say." Beneath the compassion was a hint of steel. She learned to use rifle and revolver, kept her engagements in the blitzed city even when it meant travelling by armoured car in the middle of an air raid.

She travelled half a million miles round wartime Britain with her husband, visiting factories, servicemen and bombed areas. Wrote Sir Winston Churchill to the King: "This war has drawn the Throne and the people more closely together than was ever before recorded, and Your Majesties are more beloved by all classes and conditions than any of the princes of the past."

But the constant strain had exacted a heavy toll on George VI's already frail physique. He saw Princess Elizabeth marry the Duke of Edinburgh in 1947; a year later he celebrated the twenty-fifth anniversary of his own wedding to "the most marvellous person in the world in my eyes." Soon, however, he suffered an attack of thrombosis. Then, in the autumn of 1951, his doctors diagnosed cancer, and his right lung was removed. He seemed to make a good recovery, but on February 6, 1952, six days after seeing Princess Elizabeth and the Duke of Edinburgh off on a Commonwealth tour, George VI died in his sleep at Sandringham. He left a widow who, as his friend Earl Mountbatten of Burma has said, "without in any way altering his character, made him the kind of man he wanted to be."

**New Rule.** With her daughter succeeding her as Queen, the Queen Mother had to build a new life. She quickly made it plain that she had no intention of simply retiring. In a message to the country, she wrote: "My only wish is that I may be allowed to continue the work that we sought to do together"—and no Queen dowager in Britain's history has taken such an active part in public life as she has made for herself over the past two decades.

Her travels as ambassador extraordinary have ranged the world from Europe to the West Indies,

Africa to North America, and everywhere local opinion echoes the verdict of the *New York Daily News*: "The Queen Mum is strictly OK." If royalty is a profession, she is a thorough professional who calls her magnificent gowns and jewels "my props." Lady Jean Rankin, her lady-in-waiting for 28 years, tells of the Queen Mother enchanting thousands of African tribesmen who had gathered to see her by wearing a glittering evening dress and diamond tiara in the blistering midday sun. "They've come to see a Queen," she said, "and I don't want to disappoint them."

**Light Side.** Nothing can suppress her sense of fun. She loves it when a cat strolls across a dais during an interminable speech, or a solemn councillor's bowler spins off in the wind. She has a dry wit. In South Africa, after a lunch at which a republican politician had spoken at great length about the past misdeeds of the imperialistic English, she gravely told him: "I do so sympathize. That's just how we felt about them in Scotland."

The Queen Mother still thinks of herself as a Scot. When she is in residence at Clarence House, her London home with its gas-lit cobbled courtyard and Guardsmen on sentry duty at the gates, a piper plays outside her window at nine o'clock every morning. After the King died she bought the Castle of Mey on the bleak coast of Caithness near John o' Groats, and in August usually spends her birthday there, tramping the countryside in all weathers and happily beachcombing for shells on the rocky shore.

But for most of the year her life is centred on Clarence House. This cream-painted mansion some 300 yards down The Mall from Buckingham Palace is a homely, comfortable place: the massed flowers, pleasant chintzes and corgi dogs are in keeping with a grandmother who, as well as being a connoisseur of the arts, enjoys detective novels, music hall, canasta and charades.

**In Residence.** Clarence House is run by a small staff of retired officers and ladies-in-waiting whose relaxed amiability conceals a crisp efficiency and absolute devotion to the Queen Mother. Says Sir Martin Gilliat, now in his twentieth year as private secretary: "It's absolutely fascinating working with her. No day is ever the same. She has great kindliness, but she is a perfectionist —there's an inflexible determination that standards must be high."

In many ways Clarence House reflects the Queen Mother's wide range of interests, from the cabinets of fine Chelsea china she has acquired piece by piece to the gardens where she indulges her passion for roses and flowering shrubs. She is a good judge of painting, and her 200 canvases include works by Monet, Nash, Sickert and Augustus John. There is a ticker tape to keep her in touch with racing; she has about ten horses in training and has a reputation as a knowledgeable owner. "It's her greatest enthusiasm," says Sir Martin, "after her family and friends."

The Queen Mother once remarked: "I always liked the term 'family circle.' It sounds so close, and safe, and happy." Mother and daughters keep in close touch by telephone.

There are family gatherings based at Sandringham in January and on Deeside in summer; she dotes on her six grandchildren, and friends speak of the special bond between her and Prince Charles. The admiration felt for her among the younger members of the family was perhaps best expressed by Prince William of Gloucester, who died piloting a racing plane three years ago: "She's a tremendous, superb person."

Everyone feels the same about the much-loved lady whom all Britain thinks of fondly as the Queen Mum. Her joy in living has long warmed the nation and, indeed, the world to that familiar smiling face. As one shrewd judge of royal character, Princess Marie Louise, wrote in *My Memories of Six Reigns*: "She was a perfect wife; is a perfect mother; and is truly the Queen Mother of her country."

---

NOTICE in a shop: "No dissatisfied customer is ever allowed to leave these premises."
—G. L. Brook in *Varieties of English* (Macmillan)

# Queen and People

## JUBILEE SUPPLEMENT

# Queen and People

### An anthology presenting a unique record of 25 royal years

## Accession

O N FEBRUARY 5, 1952, Princess Elizabeth and Prince Philip were in Kenya, enjoying a break during a world tour. They drove through the Aberdare Forest game reserve, about 100 miles north of Nairobi, along a road which ended at a narrow path leading to a small lake.

Without faltering, the princess walked along to the lake's-edge close by a herd of trumpeting wild elephants. Then, followed by the prince and other members of the royal party, she climbed a series of

TITLE PAGE PHOTOGRAPH: FOX PHOTOS. ILLUSTRATIONS: ERIC STEMP wooden ladders and platforms 35 feet into Treetops Hotel, a five-room observation cabin cradled on the branches of a giant tree.

That evening before dinner at Treetops the conversation turned to King George VI's illness. Concern was expressed that he had stood hatless at London Airport on a bitterly cold January morning to bid his daughter and son-in-law farewell. The princess remarked with affection: "He never thinks of himself."

She expected him to make a good recovery. But at some unknown moment during the night—perhaps while she sat on the Treetops balcony, watching the elephant, rhinoceros and waterbuck below—the King died in his sleep at Sandringham.

The visitors' book at Treetops records: "For the first time in the history of the world, a young girl climbed into a tree a Princess and climbed down the next day a Queen." [1] *

AT 25, Princess Elizabeth Alexandra Mary became the forty-second sovereign of England since William the Conqueror, and one of the seven reigning monarchs of Europe.

She was now official Head of the Church of England and titular head of Office, Law and Honour throughout a vast Commonwealth. Her subjects and citizens numbered 539 million. [2]

* For identification of sources see page 88.

PRINCE Philip, according to Michael Parker, then his private secretary, "looked as if you'd dropped half the world on him." But Queen Elizabeth II appeared very much in command of the situation. She had to show herself to her officials and servants as Queen, and she betrayed absolutely nothing.

Her work started at once. There were telegrams to be sent to those awaiting her on the next stages of the tour, in Australia and New Zealand. She drafted the apologies herself. While her staff packed, she completed the civilities of all royal visits: she presented signed photographs and small tokens to members of the game park staff—cuff-links, ashtrays, fountain pens.

By midnight she had reached Entebbe, the nearest airport that a long-range plane could use, and was in the air on her 4,000-mile journey home. She came down the aircraft steps at London Airport, a small, calm figure in black, to find the Prime Minister, Winston Churchill, waiting in the February dusk with Clement Attlee and Anthony Eden. They bowed their heads in homage to their new Queen.

Next morning at St. James's Palace, Elizabeth II held her first Privy Council.

"My heart is too full," she said in her Accession Declaration, "for me to say more to you today than that I shall always work as my father did throughout his reign, to uphold the Constitutional government and to advance the happiness and prosperity of my peoples." [3]

*Lady Longford remembers the funeral of King George VI:*

We were sitting in St. George's Chapel at Windsor, waiting for the service to begin. Suddenly the organ stopped and there was dead silence. Except for Lord Pethick-Lawrence. The old gentleman was rather deaf and hadn't noticed the silence. At the sight of the royal catafalque and the slim, almost childlike figure of the Queen—for we were high up among the grey traceries and she looked very small—he said loudly what most of us were thinking: "Charming little creature! I do hope they don't work her too hard." [4]

# Undoubted Queen

*The 16-month interval between Elizabeth II's accession and her coronation on June 2, 1953, was determined by the preference for staging the procession in the summer,* *the need to set up and finance a staff to supervise such major projects as building miles of stands—and the wish to give foreign guests time to fit the occasion into their diaries.*

THE QUEEN well understood the mystic symbolism of the coronation ceremony. Early in adolescence she had experienced her parents' devout consecration, and now she dedicated herself with similar zeal. "Pray for me on that day," she asked in the first Christmas broadcast of her reign in December 1952. "Pray that God may give me wisdom and strength to carry out the solemn promises I shall be making." [3]

IN THE hectic, hard-hammering final weeks before the Coronation, not a street or alley in the land was without its decorations. An extraordinary change came over the heart of London. Staid old buildings were engulfed in grandstands, which in turn became embowered in flowers and bunting.

Everyone with a window overlooking the five-mile procession route had a realizable fortune in prospect, and seat ticket agents discovered there was no show business like the Coronation. You could chart the fever by the profiteering —£3,500 for a side-street balcony with champagne for 50; £65 a seat for a view through the trees from Park Lane.[5]

ON CORONATION eve the Mall was packed, 12 deep, with 30,000 people bedding down with stools, spirit stoves, radios, blankets and waterproofs. It rained on them all night, but as the morning newspapers came on the streets there were unexpected headlines. Mount Everest had been conquered for the first time, and by a British team under Colonel John Hunt. Edmund Hillary, a New Zealand bee-keeper, had been the first to set foot on the summit with his sherpa, Tenzing Norkhay. It was taken as a better omen for the future than the weather, which was to continue drizzling all day in defiance of the meteorologists, who had selected June 2 as the most consistently sunny day of the calendar.

Attended by scarlet and gold-coated Yeomen of the Guard, Queen Elizabeth II arrived at Westminster Abbey with her husband in the State Coach at 11 a.m. "I was glad when they said unto me, We will go into the House of the Lord," rang out the notes of the opening anthem —and Elizabeth II stepped out on her progress down the aisle.

"Sirs, I here present unto you Queen Elizabeth, your undoubted Queen," called out the Archbishop of Canterbury as he offered her to the four corners of the Abbey: east, south, west and then north, where the foreign pressmen were sitting. This Recognition was intended only for the Queen's subjects in the Abbey, but already the atmosphere was so charged that the pressmen joined in the loud shouts of "God Save Queen Elizabeth!" [3]

*One of the British journalists present, Joan Reeder, recalls:*
The Queen, her crimson velvet

## Quotable Quotes

JANUARY 2 is when most people find that it's easier to break a resolution than a habit.

—*Farm Journal*

SUCCESS IS the child of audacity.

—Disraeli

MOST OF US would rather risk catastrophe than read the instructions.

—Mignon McLaughlin

WOMEN KEEP a special corner of their memories for sins they have never committed. —Alfred Capus, quoted by Cornelia Otis Skinner in *Elegant Wits and Grand Horizontals* (Michael Joseph)

LIBERTY is a boisterous sea. Timid men prefer the calm of despotism. —Thomas Jefferson

IT IS NOT miserable to be blind; it is miserable to be incapable of enduring blindness. —John Milton

LIFE can only be understood backwards, but it must be lived forwards. —Kierkegaard

THE ULTIMATE sin of the mind is the failure to pay enough attention.

—John Ciardi, *Dialogue With an Audience*

train carried by six Maids of Honour gowned in white and gold, moved to her Chair of Estate. The Archbishop administered the Coronation Oath:

"Will you solemnly promise and swear to govern the peoples of the United Kingdom of Great Britain and Northern Ireland, Canada, Australia, New Zealand, the Union of South Africa, Pakistan and Ceylon, and of your Possessions and the other territories to any of them belonging or pertaining, according to their respective laws and customs?"

In an unwavering voice came her reply: "I solemnly promise so to do."

The glory of Handel's music swelled about us. The Queen crossed to the high-backed King Edward's Chair. Grave and intent, the Archbishop anointed her hands, her breast, then her head with holy oil, speaking the ancient mystery: "As Solomon was anointed king by Zadok the Priest and Nathan the Prophet, so be thou anointed, blessed, and consecrated Queen over the Peoples, whom the Lord thy God hath given thee to rule and govern."

She held out her small wrists for the Armills—the bracelets of sincerity and wisdom—to be fastened round them. We stood waiting. The Archbishop had taken the great glittering crown from the High Altar. She, holding the Sceptre, emblem of power, and the Rod, symbol of mercy, waited too.

High, high, the crown rose in the

Archbishop's hands above her head. His hands gently lowered. The crown—for her life on earth—was upon the head of our Queen.

A forest of lilies bloomed into the air and sank—it was the white arms of several hundred peeresses putting on their coronets. Then a great sound was wrung from the heart of the nation: "God Save the Queen." The trumpets shrilled, the guns at the Tower of London crashed.

We shouted: "Long live the Queen! May the Queen live for ever!"[6]

IN A broadcast to Britain and the world that evening the Queen said, quietly and gently, "As this day draws to its close I know that my abiding memory will be, not only the solemnity and beauty of the ceremony, but the inspiration of your loyalty and affection." The draft text was written in advance but the last two words were added impromptu by the Queen herself.[5]

# Meeting the People

THE QUEEN, easily the best-looking First Lady in Europe, is five feet four inches tall and weighs under eight and a half stone. She has brown hair with chestnut highlights, sapphire-blue eyes, a 24-inch waist and a delicate fair skin.[7]

MOST PEOPLE on first meeting her are surprised to find how much prettier, gayer, smaller and easier to talk to she is than the newspaper page and television screen suggest.

She is lively and spontaneous; not

an intellectual, but a shrewd observer of the passing show, quick on the uptake, with an acute sense of humour.[8]

AT A PARTY on board the royal yacht *Britannia*, a photographer she likes well laughed so heartily at a joke that he dropped his glass, which shattered around the Queen's feet.

The party froze like a Bateman cartoon. She didn't even bother to look down. But that night, at a very posh do, when his flashgun failed to go off, she said out of the side of her mouth: "It just isn't your *day*, is it, Mr Reed?"[9]

WHEN SHE became Queen, she determined to be a truly twentieth century monarch. She didn't find it easy. She was a shy, retiring girl, stiff and awkward on public occasions, rarely smiling.

But once the Queen realized that it was part of her job to demonstrate to the people how the monarchy was developing with the times, she began to relax. Gradually, with Philip's help, she changed the style of her speeches.

Out went the clichés like "truly great occasion," and "believe with all conviction;" instead she used more homely, everyday language. She began to sound more human, warmer.[7]

AT A GUILDHALL luncheon to celebrate her Silver Wedding anniversary on November 20, 1972, the granddaughter of King George V, who never made jokes in speeches, began her *tour de force* with digs at her own catchphrase, so often mocked in the past by others: "I think everyone will concede that today, of all occasions, I should begin my speech with 'My husband and I.'"

Professionally flawless as regards timing and manner, the sally provoked a burst of astonished laughter and long rounds of applause which showed how far Queen and people had moved towards each other in 25 years.[4]

IN WHAT ways does the monarch actually meet the people?

Each year there are a number of "hardy annuals:" about a dozen investitures, Maundy Thursday, the Queen's Scout Parade at Windsor on Easter Sunday, the FA Cup Final, the Derby, Royal Ascot, Installations of the Orders of the Garter and Thistle, various Garden Parties, Goodwood, the Braemar Gathering, the State Opening of Parliament, the Remembrance Day Service at the Cenotaph, the Diplomatic Presentation Party, the Christmas Day broadcast.

In addition, the monarch nowadays will frequently attend the Royal Variety Performance and the Royal Film performance, some public exhibitions (like the Ideal Home Exhibition), the Second Test Match at Lords, the Badminton Horse Trials.[10]

THE MOST spectacular of the large number of military events she attends—the Queen is Head of the Army, Navy and Air Force; they owe allegiance to her, not the Government—is the Trooping the Colour, held on a June Saturday. As such it deserves suitable preparation, and the Queen spends at least an hour every morning for two weeks riding side-saddle, this being the only occasion when she rides in that style.

Besides being a great tourist attraction, the ceremony symbolizes the special position of the House-hold troops. Escorted by the House-hold cavalry, the Queen rides from Buckingham Palace up the Mall to Horse Guards Parade. As she enters the parade ground the clock strikes eleven. It is held back or advanced so she is always seen to be on time.[11]

"I'VE BEEN impressed by her stamina," says Roderick Doble, town clerk of Greenwich, who has met the Queen on four occasions. "She once took the salute at a march past of the Royal Artillery on a terribly cold day, and when she saw the soldiers couldn't wear overcoats, she took off hers."[12]

THEN THERE are the regional tours, lasting one or two days. These were begun when George V and Queen Mary visited South Wales and the

*Trooping the Colour: Queen Elizabeth rides from Buckingham Palace to Horse Guards Parade*

West Riding of Yorkshire in 1912. They have since claimed an increasingly large part of the monarch's annual duties.[10]

THIS is the story of a visit during one such royal tour, when the Queen went to Newcastle-under-Lyme to mark the eight-hundredth anniversary of the town's Royal Charter, granted in the reign of Henry II.

The visit took four months to plan and rehearse. Shopkeepers dressed their windows with royal photographs, potted plants were laid out and floral baskets hung on lamp-posts.

The sun shone as the Queen, wearing turquoise, alighted from her Rolls-Royce. Women, men, children, day trippers, shopworkers, bus drivers cheered. She met councillors and a handful of the citizenry, made a two-minute speech, walked 150 yards, chatting here and there. She spoke to one woman about shopping; then had a few comforting words for an elderly widow dressed in black, who later said: "I've just lost my husband. But now I've found a friend for life."

After 45 minutes the Queen left. And suddenly, despite—or because of—the pomp, the ceremony, the detail, the cost and all the fuss, Newcastle-under-Lyme was a much happier place.[13]

---

## Royal Exchange

PREVENTED by lumbago from playing in a golf tournament with the Duke of Windsor, Alexandre Bertrand received a sympathetic letter from the Duke, recommending his own doctor, and giving the address as Avenue Papa. Bertrand was mystified until the penny dropped—the doctor lived in Avenue George V in Paris.                    —*The Times*

## Food for Thought

A PLUMP, well-fed lion was explaining to a starving friend the secret of his success. "It's easy," he said. "All you have to do is to take a job in an office and eat a different member of the staff each day."

The second lion took this advice and for six months all went well. Then suddenly he was given the sack. Meeting his friend the next day he explained: "I made a great mistake yesterday. I ate the man who makes the morning coffee, and they soon missed him."                    —*Tit-Bits*

# Head of the Commonwealth

In 1952 the British Commonwealth covered a quarter of the earth's habitable surface, while its population exceeded a quarter of the human race. The two Rhodesias, Malta, Malaya, Singapore, Jamaica and the British West Indian Islands, Kenya, Nigeria, Uganda, Tanganyika, the Sudan, Nyasaland, Zanzibar, the Gold Coast and Somaliland were still British Colonies or Protectorates.

Today, a process begun in the reign of the Queen's father has been virtually completed, and nearly all Britain's former dominions and dependencies have been granted full independence and national sovereignty, together with generous financial and other aid.

No comparable act of liberation by the rulers of a great Empire is known to history.[14]

Queen Elizabeth II has been to Canada ten times, Australia five times, New Zealand four times, Jamaica and Fiji three times, and almost every part of the Commonwealth at least twice.

Some of these tours have been staggering in their scope. The six-month Commonwealth Tour of 1953, for example, involved the Queen and the Duke of Edinburgh in 19,307 miles of travel by sea, 17,267 by air, 3,600 by car and 1,500 by train. In 1961 there was a three-week tour of India — once the brightest jewel in the Imperial Crown—where the Queen received a reception far more complimentary than that previously dealt out to King-Emperors and their heirs.[10]

In the same year she visited Ghana —the first of Britain's black African

ILLUSTRATION REFERENCE SOURCE "ELIZABETH OUR QUEEN" BY REGINALD DAVIS, PUBLISHED BY COLLINS AT £3·95 states to achieve independence. There had been threats against the President, Kwame Nkrumah. But the Queen has never flinched from the threat of bombs and bullets. She insisted that the State drive through the darkened streets of Accra, riding in the same carriage as the President, should proceed.

Audrey Russell, the radio and television commentator who has travelled thousands of miles covering royal tours, recalls: "I was very anxious for the Queen. To carry on in those circumstances showed her enormous courage."[15]

HAROLD MACMILLAN, in fact, tried to stop her going to Ghana because of the danger. The Queen was annoyed. "Danger," she told him, "is part of the job."[11]

WHEREVER the Queen goes, that spot is momentarily the centre of the Commonwealth, and the soldier on parade, the artisan at his bench, the nurse by the bedside and the patient under her care, are enabled to feel themselves exalted by the recognition of their place in a worldwide family and a vast design.[16]

THOUSANDS of small craft in Sydney harbour greeted the Queen when she first set foot in Australia on a February day 23 years ago. In the next two months 102 speeches were made and 200 heard; 162 anthems were played, 190 gifts were received, 4,800 hands were shaken and at least 2,500 curtseys were dropped. One intensive two-day programme entailed the Queen being on her feet for 20 hours.[17]

IT WAS in Australia that Philip let slip a remark which gave some indication of his feelings. One couple presented to him were named as "Dr. and Mr Robinson." Philip raised an enquiring eyebrow and Mr Robinson hastened to explain that his wife was a Ph.D. and therefore the more important of the two of them.

"Ah, yes—we have that trouble in our family, too," commented the Prince. It was said in jest, but as so often with Philip, there was a sharp little thorn of truth hidden in the humour.[18]

AT THE start of this same tour the Queen had arrived in Auckland in drizzling rain. The people cheered her all the more when, with rain still falling, she rose to speak in her summer frock, as if refusing to acknowledge the treachery of New Zealand's summer weather. "Give her an umbrella!" they shouted, and the Deputy Mayor hurriedly stripped off his raincoat. "Thank you, Sir Walter Raleigh!" said the Queen, loud enough for the microphone to catch. And the delighted crowds acclaimed her again.[17]

RALLIES were held so that as many children in New Zealand as possible could see the Queen. After one rally,

Her Majesty related that she had overheard two small girls at the edge of the crowd arguing whether she was the Queen or Princess Margaret.

"It's Princess Margaret," said one child.

"I could not resist the impulse," said the Queen. "I leaned over and said: 'No, it's me!' "[19]

It is not generally known that the Queen and the Queen Mother have adopted several leper children, paying for all their medical and other needs. Once, when touring Eastern Nigeria, the Queen drove some miles out of her way to visit a leper settlement at Oji River. She saw, and was seen by, a thousand patients, and visited all the compounds and classes, compassionate and unflinching. The visit was noteworthy in lessening the exaggerated African fear of catching the disease.[17]

One day Her Majesty, after watching some exhilarating African ceremonies, remarked to Prince Philip: "I feel like an African Queen."

"You *are* an African Queen," he replied.[4]

# Ambassador to the World

*An official trip to a non-Commonwealth country is ranked a State Visit. Lord Chalfont, who has been the Queen's Minister in Attendance on several such visits, writes:*

To appreciate the impact of a State Visit it is essential to understand what lies behind, and what follows, it. The British monarchy occupies a unique band in the

## Quotable Quotes

TELEVISION has re-created for the great modern democracies one of the conditions of the Greek city state: all citizens can see and hear their leaders.
—Lord Brain, quoted in *The Observer*

HE WHO believes in nothing still needs a girl to believe in him.
—Eugen Rosenstock-Huessy

THE COST of a thing is the amount of what I call life which is required to pay for it, immediately or in the long run.     —Thoreau

SCIENCE has given back to the universe that quality of inexhaustible richness and unexpectedness and wonder which at one time it seemed to have taken away.     —Sir Edward Appleton

IF WE could learn how to utilize all the intelligence and patent goodwill children are born with, instead of ignoring much of it—why, there might be enough to go round!     —Dorothy Canfield Fisher

NO SNOWFLAKE in an avalanche ever feels responsible.
—Stanislaw Lec

ONE ALWAYS tends to overpraise a long book because one has got through it.     —E. M. Forster

TROUBLE: the structural steel that goes into the building of character.     —Douglas Meader

spectrum of international diplomacy. Although the Queen, as a constitutional monarch in a representative democracy, has no executive power, and does not treat or negotiate on behalf of the Government, she has for most people overseas that indefinable quality sometimes described by the overworked word "glamour."

While the Queen is walking around arid plains or cavernous museums, her Minister in Attendance may be negotiating agreements with a suitably gratified foreign minister. There is also the deep seam of goodwill to be mined by those politicians, bankers and industrialists who have the sense to take advantage of the climate of euphoria which a successful visit creates.[20]

WHEN in 1968 the Queen visited Brazil—a country where the British once had enormous investments and influence—the Brazilians were impressed by her style. She needed five aeroplanes, the *Britannia* with 230 ratings and 21 officers aboard, two frigates, 14 members of the Household, two plain-clothes police officers, seven officials, 24 staff including a Royal Pastry Chef and a Page of the Presence, and a 22-piece orchestra.

On November 1, having said good-bye to her four children, she left London Airport in a blue and white VC-10 piloted by three squadron leaders and carrying, among other goodies: 24 bottles of

Liebfraumilch Madonna, 24 bottles of Beaujolais, three tins of Dundee cake, eight boxes of After Eight mints, three jars each of strawberry and raspberry jam, 24 tins of Danish cream and three bottles of mint sauce. Instructions were relayed ahead that she didn't want to eat oysters or lobster.

There were also in the VC-10 the traditional items that are taken on every trip abroad: tea-making equipment consisting of bottled Malvern water, monogrammed electric kettle and China tea; a hot-water bottle; special feather pillows; barley sugar to suck before speeches. Polo sticks, assorted presents, 200 poppies for Remembrance Day, and other regal impedimenta, had gone in *Britannia*.[11]

FIVE HUNDRED and eighty of the 800 pressmen and women accredited to the Brazilian visit came from Rio de Janeiro alone, where the papers printed 426 photographs and 38,715 square inches of news coverage. This is equivalent to 129 whole pages, and at the then advertising rate of £700 a page was worth about £90,300.[11]

BOSTON was the big surprise during the six-day bicentennial State Visit to the USA last July. There was an almost audible sigh of relief from the trip's British planners and organizers when it became evident that neither the city's proud revolutionary heritage nor its angry Irish

had dampened the manifestly widespread desire to look at the Queen and, if at all possible, take a snapshot of her.

During a parade of the local Massachusetts "militia" reviewed by the Queen, some units were accompanied by gaggles of women and children in colonial dress. Several slowed the march past by turning to the reviewing stand and sweeping low curtseys *en masse*, and many of the mob-capped ladies plucked cameras from somewhere as they rose and took what must have turned out very blurred pictures of the royal couple before marching on.

For the Queen, there were the usual formalities — local officials, Girl Scouts (the American equivalent of Girl Guides), honour-guard reviewings, lunching and dining and changing clothes several times each day. Her speeches were variations on the theme that the 1776 Revolution was really A Good Thing leading to the peaceful evolution of Empire into Commonwealth and the enduring friendship between mother country and its former dependency.

Nor was the *Britannia*'s imposing 413-foot luxury wasted. While the Queen was in Washington, D.C., a group of American businessmen spent a day aboard the royal yacht— a term that caused much bewilderment to many spectators who were looking for something a bit smaller than 5,000 tons—talking with British businessmen and officials.[21]

A TYPICAL day during a State Visit begins at about 9 a.m. when the royal suite assembles for the first official engagement, normally at ten o'clock. From then on, every minute is accounted for in a meticulously organized programme of visits to city halls, factories, schools and department stores.

In the middle of the day there is a formal luncheon, at which the Queen is usually expected to deliver a speech. In the afternoon there are more visits—to universities, art galleries, national monuments. This goes on until the evening, when it is time to change for a reception, a formal dinner and another speech. The day seldom ends before midnight, and often much later.

Anyone who believes that the Queen looks forward to that kind of programme as enormous fun— a "junket"—must need his head examined.[20]

DURING the 1959 tour of Canada, the Queen visited an Indian village on the shores of Vancouver Island. As the royal entourage moved down the line of teepees, they were assailed by an indescribable smell, clearly emanating from a large iron pot which hung over a blazing fire in front of the last wigwam.

An elderly woman was stirring the contents of the pot, and each time she stirred, another steamy cloud wafted over the royal party, reducing members of the press corps to tears of anguish.

Her Majesty showed no sign of anything but unmitigated joy as she approached the cauldron, leaned over it, and found herself staring into a brew of fish eyes, heads, tails and bones of every description. The woman gave another stir, and the Queen almost disappeared in the billowing steam.

When it cleared, there was Her Majesty, still smiling. She turned to the woman and said warmly, "How nice!"[22]

IN AMSTERDAM during a State Visit to The Netherlands in March 1958, the Queen went to the diamond-cutting plant of the Asscher brothers, who had cut and polished the nine main pieces of the great fist-sized Cullinan diamond 50 years before; and for the first time in public Her Majesty wore the immensely valuable brooch made from two of the larger stones which she calls "Granny's chips" because the stones originally belonged to Queen Mary.

She took off the brooch, asking that the stones be shown to the one surviving partner present at the cutting. "I brought them along," she explained, "thinking that he might like to see them again." This true thoughtfulness for an old gentleman—entirely the Queen's idea— was the story of the week in the Dutch papers.[17]

ON THE State Visit to West Germany in 1965, one of her myriad

Hanoverian cousins remarked: "Stability, stability. That's what it's all about. The British don't know how lucky they are." [9]

Britain watched by television the spectacle at dusk in the gardens of the Schloss Brühl, near Bonn, when 6,000 German schoolchildren lit candles for the Queen.

Next morning the welcoming response to the royal visit was framed in a phrase in a German newspaper: "Since yesterday Germany has a Queen. She's called Elizabeth." [23]

Back in London at the end of a tour, the Foreign Secretary met the Queen at the Palace.

"It seems odd," she remarked, "to be welcomed into one's own house."

"This isn't ours," said Philip. "It's a tied cottage." [11]

# Machinery of Monarchy

When the Queen and the Duke of Edinburgh moved into Buckingham Palace at the beginning of the reign, much of it was inefficient and physically uncomfortable: there was central heating which hardly worked, laughable old telephones, and kitchens so far away from dining-rooms that food became cold on the journeys.

Today, although the frame and fashion of Nash's old building remains, much has been modernized within. The heating is oil-fired and good, the intercom systems highly sophisticated, the kitchens up to date. Electric book-keeping machines and teleprinters click busily in office and study; mechanized cost-accounting has come. Sense and streamlining are manifest at once. The footman who takes your overcoat in the Privy Purse lobby is no vision in scarlet: he is dressed in a plain navy-blue uniform with a simple "ER" cipher on the breast pocket.[8]

LIKE THE chief executive of any international company, the Queen spends many hours at a desk. After breakfast, when she and Prince Philip have discussed each other's programme for the day, she goes to her study on the first floor of the north wing of the Palace.

Usually her first meeting is with her private secretary to discuss matters demanding prompt attention. Next, with two assistant secretaries, she attends to the mail. A spate of letters arrives regularly at the Palace post office. She reads much of the mail herself; then it is dealt with by the private secretaries.

Letters vary from appeals for help from the families of people who have fallen foul of the law to the mentally unstable who misguidedly believe that a letter to the Queen will solve all ills. There are also requests from various bodies for the Queen's presence, and she accepts about one in 50. Letters in unfamiliar languages go to the Foreign Office; people in distress often have their letters forwarded to a suitable society for investigation and, if necessary, help.

The Queen also receives at her desk the many leather-covered despatch boxes containing secret and

---

## Quotable Quotes

WHEN one has much to put in them, a day has a hundred pockets.
—Friedrich Nietzsche

ANOTHER person's secret is like another person's money: you are not as careful with it as you are with your own. —E. W. H.

TACT is the art of recognizing when to be big and when not to belittle.
—B. C.

MY interest is in the future—because I'm going to spend the rest of my life there. —Charles Kettering

NOTHING so needs reforming as other people's habits. —Mark Twain

THERE'S no point in burying a hatchet if you're going to put up a marker on the site. —Sydney Harris

HAPPINESS is being married to your best friend. —Barbara Weeks

THE reason why many persons don't see things in the right perspective is that they are always looking for an angle. —T. M. E.

official documents. The quantity of papers inside the despatch boxes can depend on whether Parliament is in session—but irrespective of the volume, the boxes always follow the Queen, even when she is abroad.

On the whole, official papers fall into three categories: vital documents such as the ones empowering Commissioners to give the Royal Assent in the House of Lords (that is, the Bills which then become Acts of Parliament); routine papers which the Queen must sign—for instance, the appointment of Service chiefs; and finally, the Cabinet minutes and the despatches circulated by the Foreign and Commonwealth Office to keep the Queen informed.[24]

To SEE her reading a document is like watching a mechanical scanner at work. Her eyes flick along the lines rapidly, zigzagging down the page to complete it in a matter of seconds. But she is clearly not skimming, for she quite often trips on something that offends her logic, and then she will ask sternly: "What does *this* mean?"[25]

THE QUEEN receives numerous communications from Commonwealth countries. Their correspondence never passes through Whitehall but goes to her direct, either straight from the capitals concerned or through the High Commissioners' Offices in London. Oddly

enough, the republican countries of the Commonwealth supply the Queen assiduously with secret information even though she no longer has any legal connections with them. This illustrates why a reigning monarch after years in office becomes a store of information unmatched by anyone else in Britain.[24]

THERE is little in Britain's national life that escapes the Queen's notice. What is more, she always wants to know the reasons for the great themes of public policy; she wants to know *why*. She is interested in the substance of the policy, not merely its presentation.[26]

SHE HAS always seen herself and the serving Prime Minister as a combination of two people with separate and individual responsibilities united in a common purpose: good government, social stability, the country's well-being. In the Queen's eyes, there is a professional relationship between herself and the Prime Minister of the day; and the relationship, however friendly, is kept within those terms.

After announcing his resignation, Harold Wilson had a word of warning for his successor. "I shall certainly advise him to do his homework before his Audience, and to read all his telegrams and Cabinet Committee papers in time, and not to leave them to the weekend, or he will feel like an unprepared schoolboy."[26]

AFTER a couple of hours at her desk, the Queen embarks on the rest of her working day—perhaps a stream of public engagements, sittings for portraits, entertaining foreign guests, or some of the 200 to 300 audiences she gives each year.[27]

SHE CONTRIBUTES something solid to most conversations. Ambassadors off on new postings get devastating —and often irreverent—insights into the foreign leaders they will be dealing with, for she has met most of them personally.[25]

SINCE he was a teenager, Prince Charles has been educated to believe he must take a part in what his grandfather, George VI, called "the Royal firm." Now he and Princess Anne are taking on their own share of the ever-increasing volume of public duties.

The Queen's private life has always been precious to her. She spends as much of her free time as possible in the country, at Windsor, Sandringham or Balmoral—remote from the pomp of Buckingham Palace. A member of the Queen's household says: "She looks upon the Palace as her office, in a way. When she's there she works virtually non-stop. But in the country she is truly herself." [7]

# Royal Wife and Mother

WHENEVER possible, Saturdays and Sundays, Christmas and most of the Easter holidays are spent at Windsor Castle. It is very much a lived-in home.

Sheep and cows at the Home Farm, boats on the lake at Frogmore, polo at Smith's Lawn, dances in St. George's Hall, film shows, house-parties for Ascot—all these are part of the pattern of life at Windsor.[27]

EVEN AT Sandringham after Christmas, the Queen has her desk-work to get through every day, but both she and her mother go for long walks, whatever the weather, with their dogs. Between tea and dinner the Queen Mother plays cards or other games with her grandchildren and the Queen joins in if she has time.

In August the Royal Family gathers on Deeside, at Balmoral Castle and Birkhall. Two isolated cottages on Balmoral Estate serve as headquarters for many greatly enjoyed family picnics. The Royal Family and their guests drive themselves there, and enjoy total privacy. Sometimes they paint — Prince Philip and Prince Charles are particularly keen artists.

On chilly days they light a fire indoors and eat their picnics there. It is a rule that everything is always tidied up and the cottage swept carefully by the party themselves, before the cars set off home.[28]

To PRETEND that the Queen is a "normal" person, or even wants to be, is absurd, in spite of the headscarf, seamed stockings and "sensible" clothes. Basically, she enjoys the private life of the privileged Victorian upper class, and it is in the domestic details that she differs so much from her subjects.

Everyone likes to see their young children before they go to bed. Not everyone has had to ask the Prime Minister to delay coming round for half an hour so that she can do so.

Most people feed their pets. Not everyone feeds corgis with elegant ritual. Each evening, at about five o'clock, a footman brings into her sitting-room a tray of three dishes and several bowls. The dishes contain, separately, cooked meat, dog biscuit and gravy. A white plastic sheet is placed on the carpet. With a silver fork and spoon, the Queen dishes out portions of the food and gives it to the dogs.[11]

ONE OF the world's richest women, she hates waste. She will switch off unnecessary lights in the royal living quarters and have old carpets patched rather than buy new ones. When she was first married, she used to count her teacups every day to make sure none had been broken or chipped.[7]

How WEALTHY *is* the Queen? Royal finances are an intricate and often misleading combination of private wealth and public payments. For example the Crown Estates, which include about 250,000 good agricultural acres, much of Regent Street in London and quaint-sounding areas of England like Whaplode in Lincolnshire and Gopsall in Leicestershire, produced nearly £5 million in revenue in 1975, but this goes straight to the Government.

Whereas Prince Philip receives an annual government grant (which is taxed) of £65,000, the Queen gets no cash benefits whatever from the State. In fact, in 1975 she contributed £150,000 of her own money towards the basic £1,400,000 running costs of the monarchy (which mostly consists of the salaries of the 337 full-time and 126 part-time staff).

Ceremonial trappings of the monarchy, such as *Britannia* and the Royal Train, are all owned and paid for by the State. The Treasury Solicitor has ruled that Buckingham Palace, Windsor Castle, St. James's Palace, Kensington Palace, Hampton Court Palace, Kew Palace and Holyrood House, Edinburgh, are "non-surrenderable Crown property. They are vested in the Sovereign and cannot be alienated." In other words, they and most of the paintings and other valuables they contain belong to the Queen only as long as she is Queen.

She owns Sandringham and Balmoral, however. There is no official information about the Royal Family's other property. Once they had a great deal of property in New York, and undeveloped land in Western Canada, but much of this had to be disposed of during the Second World War.

The Queen is exempt from all taxes for, as the Inland Revenue explains: "She is Sovereign. It is part of the Royal Prerogative." She uses several stockbrokers, and her personal shareholdings, unless she has been badly advised, must be substantial. These private funds, though, she handles herself, so in order even to approximate her private wealth, it is necessary to make assumptions. But the Queen's *known* assets come to about £43 million.[29]

ALTHOUGH cosmopolitan, the Queen is lonely enough to choose as confidante a woman from a totally different background — "Bobo" MacDonald, her former nurse and spinster daughter of a Scottish railwayman — and uncomplicated enough to appoint a homoeopath, Dr. Grace Blackie, as a Household physician.

The Queen's tastes are simple and safe: Handel's *Water Music*, biography, Agatha Christie, and historical novels. She watches television a lot; likes *Dad's Army* and Dudley Moore. Her favourite hobby, fortuitously, is acting, and house guests indulge in The Game, a sort of charades race. "I looked forward to it with total horror," recalls one friend. "Imagine making a fool of yourself in front of the Queen and Prince Philip. In the event, it was one of the most enjoyable evenings I have spent." [11]

SHE IS very decisive about her clothes, and it's not easy to influence her. Hardy Amies, her dress designer, describes the situation

"In August the Royal Family gathers at Balmoral.
Here they enjoy total privacy."

graphically: "If the Queen doesn't like it, she looks at me through the mirror and raises one eyebrow. Nothing more need be said." [30]

THE DRESS designer who created Princess Anne's first long ball frock went to the Palace for a fitting. He left the room while the princess tried on the dress, and when he was shown back in again to pin it, the Queen was there. Turning from looking at his lavish creation, she enquired, "Will it wash?" [31]

THE QUEEN's cardinal interests are horsemanship and the breeding, training and management of horses. There are the ones she owns and trains at her expense (and from which she takes all winnings), and those bred by the National Stud and leased to the Queen throughout their racing life (whose winnings are shared). Her most celebrated horse was the chestnut Aureole, which won £36,225; when he went to stud at Sandringham he handsomely helped to subsidize the Norfolk estate. [24]

EVEN AT 26, she probably knew more about horses and horse-racing than any other young woman of her age. Once, when inspecting a new horse which she thought of buying, she watched him trotting for a minute or two and then drew the veterinary surgeon's attention to a flaw in the animal's breathing. "Many members of my profession would envy Her Majesty's hearing," the vet said afterwards. "The sound the horse was making would have meant nothing except to an expert. But the Queen was right." [32]

PRINCE PHILIP is part of the picture of the Queen, for they are a team and each has learnt from the other. Officially, the Prince has no position in the Constitution. But he has made himself a constant and valuable helper of the Sovereign, and has constructed a very busy world for himself. He can and does go where the Queen cannot go—but comes back to the Palace to tell her all about it, a liaison officer *par excellence*.

The Queen and her husband are complementary personalities. They match—partly because they do not always agree. But many of the consort's views *are* identical with the Sovereign's. About the bringing up of their young, for one thing. [8]

TO PREVENT Charles and Anne becoming over-impressed with their grand surroundings, they had a limited number of toys. Their clothes were let down and the seams let out to make them last longer.

Charles once lost a new dog lead at Sandringham. No one bothered about it until the Queen found out. "Did Prince Charles look for it?" she asked a member of the staff. She was told, "Yes."

"Well, he must go back tomorrow—and find it this time," replied the Queen. And he did. [33]

WHEN CHARLES was 20, his Investiture as Prince of Wales at Caernarvon Castle on July 1, 1969, was very much a family affair, despite the majestic pageantry, the silver trumpets and the awesome ceremony. A happy mother smiled down at what the Letters Patent call her "most dear son:" a proud father watched closely, a sister with a solemn face followed every word.

As the Investiture began, the Queen, like any other mother, gave small encouraging glances to her son, kneeling bareheaded before her. Gently she lifted the crown and placed it on his head, then stepped back with the suspicion of a grin as the Prince had to put up his hands and fiddle it into place. Painstakingly, she adjusted the fall of his cloak to make sure it was just right before she fastened the clasp. And with a smile that said everything was fine, she leaned forward to brush his cheek with a kiss that in the programme they call the Kiss of Fealty but, to those who watched, was simply a "well done" kiss from a mother.[34]

God Save the Queen

AT A TIME when most of the world's monarchs have either disappeared or been downgraded to figureheads, the standing of the British Crown is unique. The success of the second Elizabethan era — during which there have been considerable social, political and economic changes—is summed up by *The Times*:

"The Queen has had to face one of the most difficult periods for monarchy, a period in which almost all the trends of intellectual fashion were running against the principle of monarchy itself.

"Her weapons have been very

English ones. A certain reserve wholly appropriate to her position; a sense of humour and, above all, that common sense which the British admire more than any other quality in their public figures." [35]

SHE MUST now be ranked not only as one of the central figures on the world stage but also one of the most respected, having outlasted six US Presidents, four German Chancellors and three changes of regime in Russia. The accumulated wisdom and experience of the Sovereign is a source of real and growing value to our political leaders.[36]

*Historian Sir Arthur Bryant:*

If there has been some public disillusion during the reign with Britain's political and administrative institutions and rulers, there has been little or none with the Crown. And for this, in a jealously egalitarian age, the credit belongs to the wearer of the Crown and the devotion and efficiency with which, in the face of unceasing publicity, the Queen and the Royal Family have carried out their duties.

One reason why British constitutional monarchy has worked so well in the fast-changing third quarter of the twentieth century has been the

SOURCES: 1. *Treetops Hotel*, by Eric Sherbrooke Walker (Robert Hale). 2. *How the Queen Reigns*, by Dorothy Laird (Hodder & Stoughton). 3. *Majesty: Elizabeth II and the House of Windsor*, by Robert Lacey (Hutchinson). 4. *The Royal House of Windsor*, by Elizabeth Longford (Weidenfeld & Nicolson). 5. *The Royal Bedside Book*, by Helen Cathcart (W. H. Allen). 6. Joan Reeder in the *Daily Mirror*, June 3, 1953. 7. Frank Jeffrey in *Woman's Own*, April 24, 1976. 8. *Ten Seconds From Now*, by Godfrey Talbot (Hutchinson). 9. Vincent Mulchrone in the *Daily Mail*, February 7, 1972. 10. *The House of Windsor*, by Denis Judd (Macdonald and Jane's). 11. *The Reality of Monarchy*, by Andrew Duncan (Heinemann). 12. Interview by Hilary Macaskill in the *Observer Magazine*, April 18, 1976. 13. John Dodd in *The Sun*, June 1, 1973. 14. *A Thousand Years of British Monarchy*, by Arthur Bryant (Collins). 15. *Sunday People*, February 16, 1975. 16. *The Work of the Queen*, by Dermot Morrah (William Kimber). 17. *Her Majesty*, by Helen Cathcart (W. H. Allen). 18. *The Crown and the Ring*, by Graham and Heather Fisher (Hale). 19. *The Royal Visit to New Zealand* (A. H. and A. W. Reed). 20. Lord Chalfont in *The Times*, July 5, 1976. 21. *The Economist*, July 17, 1976. 22. Charles Lynch, *Southam News Services*, Canada. 23. *The Married Life of the Queen*, by Helen Cathcart (W. H. Allen). 24. *Queen Elizabeth II*, by Douglas Liversidge (Arthur Barker). 25. Robert Lacey in the *Sunday Times Magazine*, April 18, 1976. 26. George Hutchinson in *The Times*, April 21, 1976. 27. *Elizabeth and Philip*, by Judith Campbell (Arthur Barker). 28. *Queen Elizabeth, the Queen Mother*, by Dorothy Laird (Hodder & Stoughton). 29. Andrew Duncan in the *Telegraph Sunday Magazine*, September 12, 1976. 30. Joyce Robins in *Woman's Own*, February 21, 1976. 31. Janet Street-Porter in the *Observer Magazine*, April 18, 1976. 32. *The Queen and the Turf*, by Helen Cathcart (Stanley Paul). 33. Eric Leggett in *Sunday People*, February 9, 1975. 34. Paula James in the *Daily Mirror*, July 2, 1969. 35. *U.S. News & World Report*, July 12, 1976. 36. *The Daily Express*, April 21, 1976. 37. *More Wit of Prince Philip* (Leslie Frewin).

Queen's clear grasp of its place and purpose in the modern state.[14]

*Prince Philip:*

"The monarchy system adds gaiety to politics." [37]

IT IS the monarchy, although long divested of political responsibility, which reminds men that the political and economic differences which divide them are less real than the ties of history and common service which unite them.

The Queen does not only symbolize, and help to promote, the unity of her people. She serves to remind them of their ideals. She represents in her person and family life, and in her dedication to her public duties, the abiding virtues of hearth, home and service on the foundations of which society rests.

During her coronation she was bidden in God's name to "do justice, stop the growth of iniquity, protect the Holy Church of God, help and defend widows and orphans, restore the things that are gone to decay, maintain the things that are restored, punish and reform what is amiss and confirm what is in good order."

By the example set from the throne, by the sincerity of her self-dedication to her unique and lonely task of serving her subjects all the days of her life, the Queen is the guarantee under God that those who direct the destinies of the nation will endeavour in her name to do those things.[14]     THE END

## Quotable Quotes

ONE OFTEN contradicts an opinion when what is really uncongenial is the tone in which it was conveyed. —Nietzsche

WHENEVER man begins to doubt himself, he does something so stupid that he is reassured.
—Stanislaw Lec, *Unkempt Thoughts*

NOTHING was made in vain, but the fly came near to it.
—Mark Twain

WE ARE PROVING that man can live in outer space and at the bottom of the sea. Meanwhile, in the area between, it's getting tougher and tougher. —*Farm Journal*

NEXT TO the dog, man's best friend is the waste-paper basket.
—*Business Week*

ONE OF LIFE'S puzzling oddities is that every centenarian has either used alcohol most of his life or has let it strictly alone.
—Arnold Glasow

NONSENSE is a kind of exuberant capering round a discovered truth.     —G. K. Chesterton

FOR SHEER artistic shaping power, nothing can compare with the daily, year in, year out, gentle abrasion of the woman who, like a river, keeps flowing with an incessant, soft pressure through her man.     —R. L. Ward

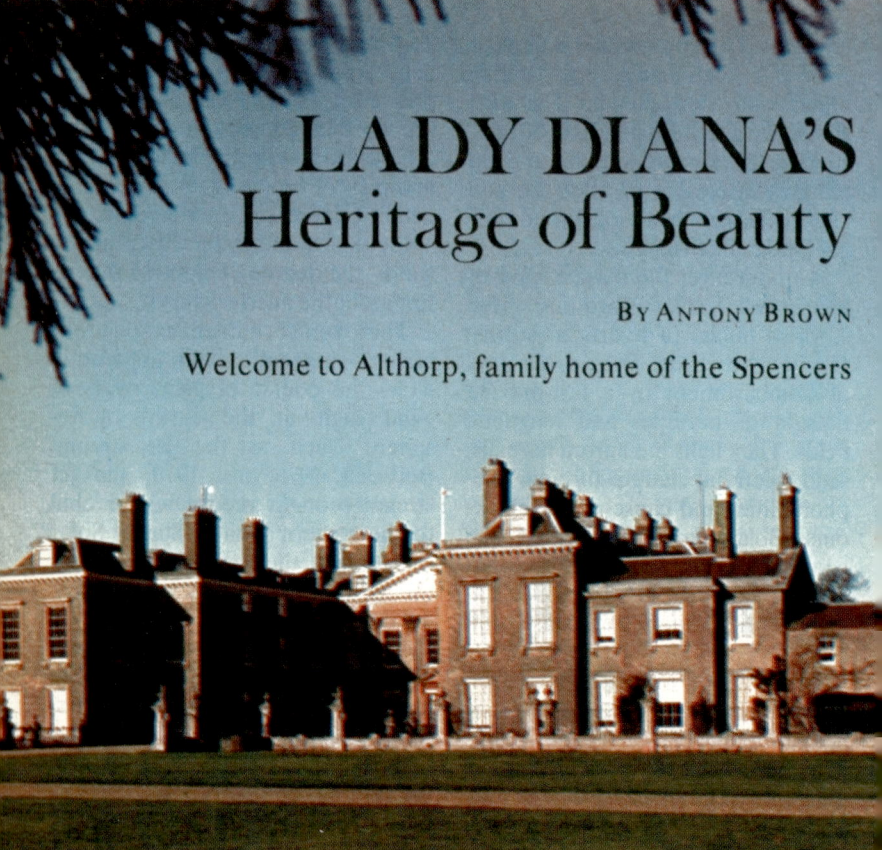

# LADY DIANA'S
# Heritage of Beauty

BY ANTONY BROWN

Welcome to Althorp, family home of the Spencers

WHEN the eighth Earl Spencer gave a dinner party for the Queen of Denmark four years ago at Althorp, his Northamptonshire country home, none of the guests who sat under the superb Venetian chandeliers in the crimson-damask dining-room could have known that they were glimpsing history—for among them was the Prince of Wales, meeting for the first time since her early childhood his future bride, Lady Diana Spencer, the Earl's youngest daughter.

Such historic moments are nothing new for Althorp, which has been the Spencer family's home for 15 generations. Nestling in 440 acres of serene parkland where deer browse as they have since the time of medieval Spencers, this gracious,

...ors frequently comment on Lady ...ana's family resemblance to her ...ebears, notably in the charcoal ...wing by John Singer Sargent of ...grandmother, Cynthia, Countess ...encer, who married the seventh ...rl in 1919 and was for 35 years ...dy of the Bedchamber to Queen ...Elizabeth, the Queen Mother

friendly house—whose treasures include one of Europe's finest private art collections—is indeed a setting for a queen.

Althorp's history chimes down the ages as melodiously as the ancient clock over its golden sand-stone stable block tells the hours of a summer's day, for Lady Diana's ancestors include statesmen, soldiers, patrons of the arts—and a galaxy of beauties who sparkle spellbindingly from the walls in canvases by Gainsborough, Reynolds, Van Dyck.

Royalty has been a frequent visitor since 1603, when James I's queen, Anne of Denmark, came to watch a masque by Shakespeare's contemporary, Ben Jonson, performed among oak trees which still stand at Althorp. Forty-four years later her son, Charles I, was playing bowls here when he learned that Cromwell's men had come to take him on the journey that was to lead to his execution. George III and Queen Victoria were both godparents to Spencer children; more recent visitors have included George V, Queen Mary, George VI and the Queen Mother.

There's nothing museum-like about this happiest, least stuffy of stately homes, where Lady Diana first went to live in 1975, when her father succeeded to the Earldom. Today village cricketers from near-by Great Brington play on the same grass where Charles I played bowls, while Althorp staff remember Lady Diana, on holiday from school near Sevenoaks, adjusting her record-player to practise ballet steps on the marble floor of the entrance hall, with its massive hunting scenes and Spencer battle honours.

In Althorp's dazzling rooms, visitors often see a Scrabble-board, a television set, or Agatha Christie paperbacks spread among the elegant eighteenth century furniture, while family photographs mingle with prized paintings and rare china.

Recalled one Althorp guide: "When they were younger, Lady Diana and her sisters would often look up from playing draughts or cards to smile at visitors filing past them."

The Spencer dynasty first flowered back in medieval times, when Sir John Spencer—he traced his line to Robert Despencer, steward to William the Conqueror—bought the estate and ancient moated house of Althorp. His grandson, another Sir John, built up a herd of some 14,000 sheep on Althorp's low hilly pastures. They fared so well that by 1603 his descendant Robert, created Baron Spencer by James I, was declared to have more ready cash than anyone in the kingdom.

It was Robert's son William who brought home to Althorp the first of its legendary beauties—Lady Penelope Wriothesley, daughter of Shakespeare's patron the Earl of Southampton. The Spencer flair for choosing stunning brides continued with her son Henry: created Earl of Sunderland by Charles I, he was married at the age of 19 to the beautiful girl he called his

The Great Staircase rises out of Saloon, where portraits of seventee and eighteenth century royal ladies I the right-hand wall. It was built of c around 1650 at the command of the lov Sacharissa—Dorothy, Countess of Sunderla (left), here painted by Sir Anthony Van Dy born Lady Dorothy Sidney, she added to Spencers the lineage of such legendary herc as Sir Philip Sidney and Harry Hotsp

"dearest heart," Lady Dorothy Sidney. Van Dyck loved to paint her, and the courtier-poet Edmund Waller—he called her "Sacharissa," meaning sugar-sweet—addressed ravishing love poems to her.

Sadly the Earl, fighting for the Royalist cause, was killed by a cannon-ball at Newbury in 1643; living on till 1684, his widow made the house a refuge for Royalist clergy. Some years later, Sir Richard Steele lamented in the *Tatler*: "The fine women they show me nowadays are at best but pretty girls to me, who have seen Sacharissa."

Transforming Althorp's Elizabethan simplicity into what one shrewd visitor called "the best-planned country seat in the kingdom," the second Earl of Sunderland commissioned an architect to enlarge and embellish the original house in Italianate style, and hired Le Nôtre, the great French landscape gardener who planned the gardens at Versailles, to plant chestnuts, oaks, and the avenue of elms which still stretches away from the front of the house through the park. Capability Brown, coming a century later, judged the planning so fine that it could hardly be improved on.

Le Nôtre's finishing touch, the

...ning her in Althorp's galaxy of ...auties are (left to right): Georgiana, ...e of the first Earl Spencer, affectionately ...rtrayed by Joshua Reynolds in 1759–61 with ...r young daughter Georgiana, who ...came Duchess of Devonshire; Lavinia ...igham, who married the second Earl, ...nted by Reynolds in 1785 when she was 23; ...d the fifth Earl's wife Charlotte—known as ...pencer's Fairy Queen"—painted by John ...slie in the mid-nineteenth century

Oval Lake, is one of Lady Diana's favourite spots. Weekending from her job in a London nursery school last year, she would often climb from the lake to the Jacobean Falconry, where her forebears used to watch their husbands hawking.

In 1700 the renowned name of Marlborough was linked to that of Spencer when Charles, the future third Earl of Sunderland, married Lady Anne Churchill, daughter of the great Duke: through Lady Anne, their son Charles succeeded to the Marlborough title and took the Sunderland title with him. A kinswoman of Sir Winston Churchill through the Marlboroughs, Lady Diana is also related to George Washington, one of whose forebears married

The Rubens Room, its walls covered with yellow silk damask, contains some of the paintings acquired by Lavinia, wife of the second Earl—who sold her jewellery to buy them as a commemoration of her happy marriage. Over the chimney-piece is a seascape by Henrik Dubbels; to its right, a Rubens portrait of Elizabeth of France. At the far end, visible beyond a 1757 terrestrial globe, is the Spencer family's sitting-room, known as the Long Library.

a sixteenth century Spencer. Romance flowered again at Althorp in 1755, when John Spencer, later created first Earl Spencer, married his childhood sweetheart Georgiana Poyntz. Waiting till his family were celebrating his twenty-first birthday in the ballroom, he and Georgiana slipped upstairs to be secretly married by his former tutor.

Their daughter Georgiana, who

became Duchess of Devonshire, was the most resplendent of Althorp's ladies. Known as the "Duchess of Dimples," she ruled London fashion, was whispered to be the favourite of the Prince of Wales—and caused a scandal in 1784 when, to secure the re-election of Whig leader Charles James Fox, she entered slum houses in Long Acre, exchanging kisses for votes.

It was the second Earl who gave Althorp the appearance it has today; he commissioned architect Henry Holland, who refurbished Carlton House for the Prince of Wales, to remodel it as a Georgian mansion. As First Lord in the days of conflict that led up to the Napoleonic Wars, he burnt Admiralty candles late into the night, awaiting news of Nelson.

Spencers have often guided England's fortunes. The most endearing Spencer politician was "Honest Jack Althorp," later the third Earl. Considered shy and awkward at school, his main interest lay in country pursuits. But family custom compelled him to enter Parliament—he feared going there "as if I was going to execution." Once, powerfully attacked by an Opposition member, he fumblingly replied that he had lost the notes he needed for his answer: such was the House's regard for "Honest Jack Althorp's" integrity that he still won his vote.

His deep concern to help those less fortunate made him a leading Radical. In 1830 he was offered the Premiership, which he declined. But he accepted the offices of Chancellor of the Exchequer and Leader of the House of Commons, and promoted the Reform Bill in 1832.

When he succeeded to the Earldom in 1834, he returned to his beloved estates, rearing his prized breed of shorthorn cattle and working for the Royal Agricultural Society which he helped found. At the end of his life, feeling an obligation to add to the family portraits, he commissioned 27 paintings—of his favourite shorthorn cattle.

Lovingly created and embellished over the centuries, Althorp's atmosphere is unique. Like royalty itself, it has the happy knack of combining dignity with charm, humour and unerring style. For Lady Diana herself—a "natural queen," say villagers who remember her serving in the tea-shop or visiting old people on the estate—Althorp's wedding gift is its happy heritage of beauty.

One hundred and fifty years ago this year, one of her forebears, the second Earl, gave thanks on his golden wedding anniversary for "half a century of blessings" in his marriage to Lavinia Bingham. It will be that, and more, that Althorp wishes its own princess for her wedding.

PHOTOGRAPHS: PAGE 91, LORD SNOWDON/CAMERA PRESS, LONDON;
PAGES 92, 93 AND 94, BEEDLE AND COOPER PHOTOGRAPHY

THOUGH the human tongue weighs practically nothing, it is surprising how few people are able to hold it. —William Arthur Ward

# The Queen's Birthday Spectacular

By Peter Browne

With precision, pageantry and a cast of 1,600,
Trooping the Colour is an unbeatable display

At one minute to 11 on the morning of the second Saturday in June, the Queen rides across the gravelled square of London's Horse Guards Parade and turns to face rigid ranks of soldiers in scarlet tunics and black bearskins.

As Big Ben begins to sound the hour, the Guards present arms with the crash of hands meeting rifles.

From distant Hyde Park a 41-gun royal salute booms out. Five military bands strike up the national anthem, and the stage is set yet again for Trooping the Colour, mounted in celebration of the Queen's official birthday.

To an annual television audience of seven million in Britain and many more overseas, it is the finest parade in the world, a military spectacular with a cast of 1,600. And it is the Queen's favourite ceremony, too. One rain-soaked Saturday, officials at Buckingham Palace urged her to cancel. Looking down from a window at the Guardsmen lining her processional route along the Mall to Horse Guards Parade, and the crowds waiting patiently to see her ride by, she said: "If they can stand it, so can I."

**Proving Ground.** As Colonel-in-Chief of all seven Guards regiments, no one knows better that for them the Trooping is a hallowed tradition. "You can't call yourself a Guardsman," veterans insist, "until you've done a Queen's Birthday Parade."

First held in 1805, it centres on an army custom which can be traced back for 300 years: "trooping"—carrying—a unit's flag, or Colour, down the ranks at the end of a day's march to make sure every soldier could recognize it as a rallying point in battle. The Colour, richly embroidered with battle honours, came to represent the spirit of a regiment. Each year one of the five regiments of Foot Guards—Grenadier, Coldstream, Scots, Irish and Welsh—now takes its turn to troop its Colour, its most revered possession, at the Birthday Parade.

Since the time of Charles II, the Guards have been the Sovereign's personal troops, responsible for protecting the Royal Family; hence their title of the "Household Division." In their ceremonial role, they have long contributed to British pageantry: no

right-thinking tourist would miss the daily changing of the guard at Buckingham Palace or in Whitehall, no state visit is complete without a Sovereign's Escort of the Household Cavalry.

But ceremony is only part of the Guardsman's job. Beneath the splendid uniforms are tough operational soldiers, who alternate between tours of duty at home and overseas. At least half the Guards' strength of 8,000 officers and men is normally on active service, anywhere from Germany to Cyprus, Ulster to Hong Kong.

Last year, men of the Scots and Welsh Guards who were to have taken part in Trooping the Colour were withdrawn for more urgent business elsewhere: the Household Division suffered 53 killed and 139 injured in the Falklands, and nearly 1,000 now wear the South Atlantic medal.

Many of them will be on parade at this month's Trooping—climax of a hard spell of training which begins each year in March with "Spring Drills." Explains Garrison Sergeant-Major Alexander Dumon: "The idea is to bring everyone up to fine pitch again after the winter. It's like putting a car in for a yearly service."

Nobody escapes. Cooks and clerks turn out, and officers, too, to polish their arms drill and ceremonial marching: quick time, 116 paces to the minute, slow time 65, an NCO striding alongside with a "pace stick" like a giant pair of dividers to ensure absolute accuracy. There is always one slow march past during the

Birthday Parade. Legend has it that on one occasion officers tottered on parade after an all-night party, and the officer in command ordered a slow march to disguise their unsteadiness.

By April, each Regimental Sergeant-Major has picked out the two "Guards" of 70 men he will need for the Trooping. Now he begins to weld them into teams moving as one—fully familiar with the sequence and commands of the parade, well before they come together with the other regiments for the first full-scale rehearsal.

No detail is overlooked. On the day of the parade they will have to stand motionless for up to half an hour, and a man who faints without good medical reason may find himself on a charge. A tight uniform can cause fainting, so every tunic is individually tailored, at around £240 for a soldier, £1,300 for an officer—whose hand-sewn gold embroidery alone costs some £500.

**Top-Heavy.** Fit is just as important for the Guards' 20-inch tall bearskins, copied 168 years ago from those worn by French Grenadiers captured at Waterloo. Officers' bearskins are made from the soft female fur, soldiers' from the coarser male hide, both mounted on wicker frames. Too loose, and they tilt to spoil the symmetry of a rank of marching men; too tight, and a splitting headache is a certainty. To get accustomed to the unwieldy headgear, soldiers wear bearskins with everyday khaki while drilling on the barrack square, and some officers at their desks wear them perched above civilian suits.

The pace quickens in May, with all seven regiments perfecting their own parts in a performance which depends on split-second timing. Its impresario is the Brigade Major of the Household Division, its director the Garrison Sergeant-Major, and like any other show, it has its stars.

**Behind the Scenes.** For some time beforehand, the Queen practises riding side-saddle in the Royal Mews behind Buckingham Palace. By June Colonel Andrew Duncan, in command of the 1983 parade, will also have spent hours there on horseback, rehearsing the sequence of orders and strengthening his voice by shouting them at the Mews walls.

Lieutenant Greville Bibby, aged 21, will have been equally busy at the Hounslow barracks of the 1st Battalion Grenadier Guards, whose Colour is to be trooped this year. His is the awesome task of carrying the Colour down the ranks of Guards and past the Queen. To handle with a flourish the fringed and embroidered crimson silk flag, which on its "pike" weighs some 16 pounds, takes much practice under the critical eye of the regimental sergeant-major, using a pike weighted with small sandbags.

A couple of miles away in Hyde Park there will have been training, too, for the mounted Sovereign's Escort of 122 officers and men who accompany the Queen on her three-quarter-mile ride from the palace to Horse Guards Parade. Drawn from the two cavalry regiments of the Household Division, the Life Guards and the Blues and Royals, they switch like all Guards between ceremonial duties at home and service abroad —in their case, with Chieftain tanks and the Scorpion light tanks which the Blues and Royals used so successfully in the Falklands.

Every year horses new to ceremonial are schooled at Windsor, then in Hyde Park they run the gauntlet of a Guards "rent-a-crowd" —cheering men waving flags and blowing bugles—to condition them to the crescendo as they escort the Queen.

Among the horses this year will be a veteran of many Troopings: old Sefton, fully recovered from the wounds he received last year when an IRA bomb wrought terrible carnage among a detachment of Household Cavalry riding out of their barracks. Sefton, with a white blaze, will be easily recognizable among the Sovereign's Escort—as will Coriolanus, the massive drum horse of the Household Cavalry's mounted bands, who carries two priceless silver drums presented by William IV in 1830.

**Keeping Time.** Military music makes the Trooping go with a swing, and at Chelsea Barracks the massed bands of the five Foot Guards regiments have been practising their role in a ceremony that calls for 360 musicians to play on the march, 20 abreast and 18 ranks deep, while performing drill manoeuvres. Enter again Garrison Sergeant-Major Dumon, to make sure their marching matches their musicianship and to teach the five drum majors to handle their staffs with appropriate swagger.

By the end of May, Foot Guards, cavalry and bands have all practised separately on Horse Guards Parade, where scaffolding stands for spectators have sprung up around three sides of the square. Now, with a fortnight to go, they come together for the first time in a full dress rehearsal, when seats are free. A week later comes another, costing £3 to watch. Video cameras record the entire ceremony for critical analysis by the Brigade Major and his staff, who are well aware of the Queen's close interest.

"Her Majesty has an eye for detail," notes an officer. "If she spots something wrong on the day, she will certainly tell us. It keeps everybody on their toes."

The night before the Parade every Foot Guard spends at least an hour on his kit, polishing boots, whitening belts, brushing out his bearskin and wrapping it in a damp towel to preserve its pear shape. The cavalry of the Sovereign's Escort need much longer. The underground store at their Hyde Park barracks holds some £9 million worth of magnificent ceremonial equipment for men and horses.

It takes a trooper a good three hours to clean his plumed helmet, thigh-high jackboots, buckskin breeches, glittering cuirasse, or breastplate, and the leatherwork of the harness. As many hours go into grooming his horse on the day of the Trooping.

While the cavalry labour in the

stables, coach-loads of Foot Guards are leaving their barracks at Pirbright, Caterham and Hounslow to converge on Chelsea Barracks, where to reduce the risk of fainting they are issued with barley sugar and brisk advice: "If you feel like keeling over, flex your knees, wiggle your toes, and think what the regimental sergeant-major will do to you." Every contingency has been allowed for: stretcher parties and medical orderlies, horse-boxes and vets, even trucks loaded with capes in case of rain.

**Full House.** At 9.45 the first detachment, led by its regimental band, swings through Chelsea on the two-and-a-half-mile march to Horse Guards Parade, where every £5·50 seat has long been sold. So heavy is demand that the applications to Household division headquarters in Whitehall can outnumber places by ten to one, and tickets are balloted for between January and March.

With unfailing courtesy, staff officers turn down requests for block bookings—two seats each is the rule —and persuade baffled Arabs that even £500 in cash cannot buy a ticket outside the ballot. The Guards make no profit from their biggest parade: every penny goes to pay for erecting the tiered stands.

By 10.45, all is ready. More than 7,000 spectators, among them the Prime Minister and foreign diplomats, wait expectantly; 1,000 soldiers and musicians stand in crisp formation on the parade-ground, another 400 line the Mall to Buckingham Palace. The sound of distant music from the Household Cavalry mounted bands swells as the Sovereign's Escort clatters and jingles down the Mall and into the narrow approach road to Horse Guards Parade.

There, in June 1981, a youth in the dense crowd fired six shots. The Queen calmly soothed her horse and rode on. A Guardsman presenting arms by the roadside lowered his rifle long enough to grab the gunman and hand him to police, and then, poker-faced, presented arms again. Neither he nor the Queen knew that the pistol had been loaded with blanks—but neither would allow anything to spoil their very special day.

**Order of Events.** Its time-honoured sequence never varies. The Queen, in the uniform of the regiment whose Colour is to be trooped, inspects the parade. Then the Colour is slowly and reverently carried along the ranks. The Foot Guards march past in slow and quick time; the Household Cavalry ride by at the walk and at the trot. Finally the Queen, preceded by the bands, rides back to the palace at the head of a long column of Guards.

The Trooping, that stirring, swash-buckling ceremony of precision and pageantry, is over for another year.

PHOTOGRAPHS: PAGES 98 AND 99, ANTHONY EDGEWORTH, FROM "THE GUARDS," PUBLISHED BY AURUM PRESS AT £12·95; PAGE 99 (INSET), TONY DRABBLE/CAMERA PRESS

# Who Goes to the Queen's Garden Party?

By Philip Blake

For the guests taking tea at the Palace,
it is an unforgettable afternoon

MINGLING with the throng at a Buckingham Palace Garden Party, the Prince of Wales approached Charles Cole and asked: "What do *you* do?" Polite royal interest turned to frank delight when Cole, who had been invited to represent the show business union, Equity, explained that professionally he was a clown and "balloonologist," rejoicing in the stage name Windy Blow.

Encouraged by Prince Charles, he dug a brace of balloons from his pocket, inflated them, and gave an impromptu Royal Variety Performance—twisting the balloons together to make comic animals, then helping a gleeful Charles try his hand, without much success. As the Prince moved on, with an embarrassed aide clutching a rubber dog and swan, he smiled at Cole: "You'll have to teach me to do this."

Among the most relaxed gatherings in the Queen's calendar, the three London garden parties held each July bring some 24,000 people to the palace: MPs and midwives, captains of industry and country clergymen, soldiers, surgeons and diplomats of many nations. Many are ordinary folk invited in recognition of their service to country or community, like Humberside road sweeper Ben Railton, who in 1983 accompanied the Mayor of Beverley as a reward for keeping the town's streets clean for 30 years.

Ben's invitation came from the Lord Chamberlain, who since Queen Victoria held the first royal garden party in 1868 has been responsible for organizing the biggest social events of the year. In March, hundreds of letters go out under his name to the Lord Lieutenant of each county, the heads of the armed and civil services, and such bodies as town councils and voluntary organizations, asking them to nominate a specified number of guests.

Others are chosen more directly. An invitation went to a Plymouth

teacher whose class thought so highly of her that when she retired they wrote to the Queen; another to gypsy Tom Lee, founder and secretary of the Romany Guild, who was convinced, until reassured by a solicitor, that it must be a practical joke.

The paperwork is formidable. All guests get a preliminary note asking them to select their preferred party date, but their choice of company is strictly limited to "spouses and un-married daughters over 18"—a leg-acy of the days when debutantes were presented at court. A school-boy unable to go with his mother wrote in protest to the Queen: "Isn't this breaking the Sex Discrimi-nation Act?"

**Special Delivery.** About 8,000 people accept for each party. In April the Lord Chamberlain's of-fice takes on extra staff to hand-write the invitations, and by June mantel-pieces all over the country boast handsome six-by-eight-inch cards bearing the royal cipher in gold and the ringing announcement: "The Lord Chamberlain is commanded by Her Majesty to invite . . ."

For most guests, the first problem is what to wear. Men are offered a choice of "morning dress, uniform or lounge suit." Many plump thankfully for their best suit, but Moss Bros of Covent Garden still hire out some 2,000 morning dress outfits for each party, at a topper-to-toe price of around £38.

Wives learn that "ladies wear afternoon dress (with hat) or national costume"—and, as the Princess of Wales has shown, can go bare-legged on the palace lawns with perfect propriety. High street head-gear can hardly compete with that of the more colourful overseas guests. A Cree Indian woman turned up in full ceremonial tribal dress with a single magnificent eagle's feather in her hair—by courtesy of a gallant bird at London Zoo.

The invitation card says 4-6pm, but soon after lunch harassed police in central London are already trying to sort out traffic jams, as fum-ing workaday drivers tangle with guests converging on Buckingham Palace—their cars identifiable by the large orange "X" windscreen label, issued with invitations, which allows them to park for the afternoon on normally sacrosanct territory beneath the trees along Con-stitution Hill and The Mall.

By the time the gates open at 3.15, a long queue of party-goers is shuffling towards the palace: self-conscious men with grey toppers crammed over their ears, women in flowered frocks struggling to anchor picture hats against the wind, while an irrepressible street photo-grapher cajoles, "How about one for the family album?"

**In Crowd.** The queue winds through the gates and across the forecourt, doing its best to look nonchalant beneath the fascinated gaze of tourists pressed against the palace railings. Bolder souls have made their own interpretation of the windscreen label's reference to "chauffeur-driven cars." Among the Daimlers and Rollses gliding in to set down guests on the forecourt are a number of unpretentious family hatchbacks, even a homely Mini, decanting a couple chauffeured by their beaming son.

The jauntiest arrivals in recent years must surely have been actress Diane Hart and her two daughters, who swept past the astonished sentries on their battered bikes.

The guests progress through the Grand Entrance and into the Marble Hall, with its gilt and gold leaf, its expanse of red carpet. A last short stretch across the curved pink-and-cream Bow Room, lined with cabinets of priceless Chelsea porcelain, out through the French windows on to the terrace, and there below is the Queen's garden.

**Costume Drama.** Most guests join the crowd milling beneath the terrace on one of the largest lawns in the country, to await the arrival of the Queen. Morning suits rub shoulders with flowing Arab robes, bemedalled tunics, gorgeous saris, royal red cassocks for the Queen's Chaplains and episcopal purple. A bishop, catching an amused glance at his antique gaiters, explains: "I feel it is good to give them an occasional airing against the moth."

The Queen's bodyguard of the Yeomen of the Guard, splendid in their scarlet Tudor uniforms, clear several lanes through the crowd and stand every few yards, long pikes at the ready. On the dot of four o'clock, as a band strikes up the national anthem, the Queen and members of her family appear on the terrace, then descend to stroll singly along the lanes marked by the impassive Yeomen, while guests crane their necks to spot familiar faces. "Isn't she small!" "Who's that? Prince Michael?" "Where's Diana?" A glimpse of billowing blue chiffon and

white parasol: "Look! The Queen Mum!"

The royals make slow progress, stopping often to talk to guests selected earlier from the crowd by Gentlemen Ushers and herded unobtrusively to the right spot at the right time. Among them, at a party just before the royal wedding in 1981, was a blind woman who had asked to touch the future Princess of Wales's engagement ring: at the same party, so many well-wishers brought flowers for the Princess that her detective had to put some in his topper.

The ushers, distinguished retired officers wearing carnations with their morning suits, make their choice more or less at random. One guest, supposing to an usher that everything was pre-arranged, was told, "Not at all, my dear chap. Would you like to meet the Prince?"

Last year the Mayor of Thamesdown, retired lorry driver Harry Garrett, found himself deep in conversation with the Queen about the problems of the British Rail engineering workshop in his home town of Swindon. Harry and his wife were charmed: "She put us completely at ease. We might have been chatting to a neighbour over the garden fence."

It is usual for the Queen to choose the topic of conversation; practice has perfected the art of tailoring that conversation to just the right length. One guest thought it more than coincidence that when the Queen gently swung her umbrella behind her back, an usher hastened to lead her on to the next guest.

Rarely are brollies opened, for garden parties have a knack of falling on the hottest days of the year. Sun and excitement prove too much for some: a St John Ambulance tent stands in a corner, with a mobile cardiac unit parked near by, staffed by doctors and nurses in radio contact with stretcher parties strategically stationed around the gardens. On a scorching afternoon they may scoop up perhaps 20 fainting cases.

**Tea Time.** As the royals chat their way through the crowd, it dissolves behind them. Thirsty queues form at the long tent at the side of the lawn, where knowledgeable folk have already staked a claim to the limited number of tables outside. Guests are served by hand-picked waitresses—notably Nell Jolliffe, who has completed half a century of helping at more than 150 garden parties, and has been honoured with the Royal Victorian Order by the Queen.

For the caterers, J. Lyons of Corner House fame, the parties involve around 650 staff, months of preparation, and provision of refreshments on a truly heroic scale. The 8,000 guests at each party get through an estimated 13,000 sandwiches, 10,000 bridge rolls, 4,000 baps, 5,000 strawberry tarts, 6,000 ices, 7,000 pieces of gâteau, 9,000 pastries. They drink about 800 gallons of hot and iced coffee or tea, poured from elaborate urns that are filled from the palace water supply, which is constantly checked by the Laboratory of the Government Chemist.

The guests tuck in with a will. A brigadier takes an appreciative bite of the chocolate cake whose fame has spread throughout the world. Report has it that handbags lined with grease-proof paper carry off royal goodies as souvenirs, and a few teaspoons find new homes.

The Queen's leisurely stroll across the lawn lasts about an hour. By 5.15 she is in the open-sided royal marquee enjoying her own tea, well deserved by a hostess whose garden party bill this year will top £150,000. In a scene curiously reminiscent of a medieval court, her every move is scrutinized by hundreds of guests in chairs ranged in a semicircle round the royal enclosure.

As she moves on to the VIP marquee where foreign diplomats wait to be presented, less distinguished folk eagerly explore the palace grounds. Carefully hidden among the trees are toilet tents with cologne and hairbrushes at the ready on Victorian dressing-tables. There are rose gardens to admire, stocked with *Peace*, *Silver Lining* and *Queen Elizabeth*; the blaze of colour from the spectacular 500-foot-long herbaceous border, where delphiniums are in full flower.

The garden is surprisingly big— just under 40 acres—and remarkably peaceful. High walls mute London's traffic to a distant rumble, a carefully planted avenue of chestnut trees partially screens the city's skyline. It is home to well over 200 varieties of wild plants, as well as several hundred species of butterfly and moth and some 20 species of birds —notably the rosy pink flamingos which for more than 20 years have paddled stilt-legged in the placid waters of the palace lake, enjoying an occasional treat of shrimp from a local fishmonger.

The great lawn that takes such a hammering from thousands of feet is a mixture of grasses with patches of camomile—and, surprisingly, daisies. On it stands a massive imperial trophy, the 15-foot Waterloo Vase, carved for Napoleon from a single block of marble but presented after Waterloo to George IV. At the opposite end of the garden, another reminder of the past: a black mulberry bearing a label which notes that it was planted by James I in 1609—long before Buckingham Palace was built in this corner of St James's Park.

For guests there is still time to sit beside the miniature cascade tumbling into the lake; to listen to the bands, stationed on either side of the lawn, which take it in turns to play jaunty selections of popular tunes. "Shall we go now?" a woman asks her daughter, when Big Ben strikes six and the Queen retires to the palace. "Not yet," the girl insists. "I'm going to make the most of this."

Everyone feels the same. They linger until discreetly ushered towards the exits, reluctant to end an afternoon to remember. One guest who will certainly never forget is Charles Cole, alias Windy Blow. He was invited back to the palace by Prince Charles to instruct him in the finer points of balloonology, invaluable for the father of two young sons. "Very, very promising," reports the tactful clown. "I was particularly pleased with his giraffe."

PHOTOGRAPHS: PAGE 102, TIM GRAHAM; PAGE 103, JOHN SHELLEY

---

## Snap Judgement

WHEN the announcement was pinned on the notice-board of the impending arrival of the college photographer, the girls buzzed with excitement planning what they would wear. I assured them that the photographs would be head and shoulder shots so there would be no need to get dressed up.

The next morning one pretty student came to me in a state of great agitation. "Look at me," she wailed, indicating her faded blue jeans and scuffed gym shoes. "You said they would just take pictures of our heads, but they're going to take full-length photos. It says so on the notice." We made a quick trip to the notice-board where, with a look of utter despair, she pointed to the line . . . "Photos will be taken of the entire student body."

—Margaret Last

# PRINCESS ANNE FINDS A ROLE

### By David Moller

Refusing to be 'just a figure-head or
a name on a piece of notepaper,' she
brings her own distinctive blend of
dash and determination to her work

L AST January 18 could hardly have
been worse for travel. Princess
Anne was scheduled to go by
helicopter and then by aeroplane from
her home, Gatcombe Park in Gloucestershire, to the rededication ceremony of the
frigate HMS *Amazon* in Devonport, near
Plymouth.

It soon became clear, however, that with
snow falling heavily the first leg of her

journey was out; visibility was too poor for low-level flying. This was just the sort of challenge on which Princess Anne thrives. "We'll drive," she announced.

At the wheel of her Reliant Scimitar sports car, and accompanied by her personal detective, she just managed to make her escape from Gatcombe before it was cut off by snow-drifts. In shocking conditions she drove the 20 miles to RAF Lyneham, in Wiltshire, to board an Andover of the Queen's Flight.

**Royal Progress.** On arrival at Exeter airport they met another hitch. Here, too, the weather was too bad for the planned helicopter hop to Devonport. "What sort of transport have we got?" enquired the Princess. Minutes later, she was bucketing through the snow towards Plymouth in a police Range Rover.

Finally, a beaming Princess Anne strode into a drill hall at Devonport—just 20 minutes late. As *Amazon*'s captain Commander John Ellis said later, "The Princess persevered through what must have been one hell of a journey. She used everything except a sleigh to get here."

Three weeks later, in Germany visiting a regiment of which she is Colonel-in-Chief, the 14th/20th King's Hussars, she embarked on what has become a regular highlight of such trips. Her trim five-foot-seven figure kitted out in her specially-tailored khaki tanksuit, she eased herself into the driver's seat of a 50-ton Chieftain tank.

With practised ease, she jammed her right foot down to engage the tank's 750-horsepower engine. Then, a look approaching ecstasy on her face, Princess Anne roared off across the North German plain. On a previous army visit she had once sighed, "I wish someone would give me a tank for Christmas."

Somewhat superfluously, Princess Anne has declared, "I never was a fairy-tale princess—and I never will be." But the 35-year-old Princess, sixth in line of succession to the throne, has certainly become very much a working princess; in 1984 her 501 official engagements were exceeded only by the Queen's 512 and Prince Philip's 536.

She is Colonel-in-Chief to eleven British, Canadian, Australian and New Zealand regiments, Chancellor of London University, President of the British Olympic Association, Chief Commandant of the Women's Royal Naval Service, Patron of the Riding for the Disabled Association, President of The Save the Children Fund. In all, she holds positions with 75 organizations.

To all her duties she brings her own distinctive blend of dash and determination—and at times, no little courage. Opening a new £5·5 million harbour complex at Portavogie in Northern Ireland last May she noted that, despite stringent security and minimal advance publicity, hundreds of people had gathered to cheer and wave flags.

The official schedule went out of

the window as the Princess strode over to chat to the crowd for 20 minutes. It was the closest thing to a royal walkabout the citizens of Northern Ireland had enjoyed since the "troubles" started in the late 1960s.

To organize her crowded calendar, the Princess has a staff of three working from a second-floor suite of rooms in Buckingham Palace. The fourth member of her official staff—a dresser to help with the bewildering succession of dresses and uniforms—is based at Gatcombe Park. Their wages, and Princess Anne's travel costs and dress allowance for official duties, must be met from the annual £120,000 she receives from the Civil List agreed by Parliament.

In recent years the Princess has probably won most acclaim for her work as President of The Save the Children Fund. The Fund, founded in 1919 to aid children starving in Europe in the aftermath of the First World War, now has a massive range of projects in 57 countries, from emergency relief work to nutrition and health-care programmes and the training of local workers. Here in Britain it runs more than 100 child-care projects.

Princess Anne accepted the presidency of the Fund in 1970 only on condition that she be "a *working*

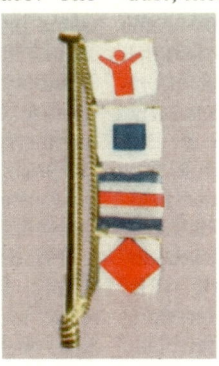

*Princess Anne's brooch (see cover) spells out SCF in flag code, under the Fund's emblem*

head—not just a figure-head or a name on a piece of notepaper." And latterly she has pioneered something new in royal travel with a gruelling series of journeys to visit Fund projects. Trekking through many of the world's poorest quarters in working clothes of denim skirt, cotton blouse, suede ankle boots and bush hat, she has endured blistering heat, dirt, dust, flies, swamps, jungle, desert.

Field-workers who meet her on these trips are amazed at her grasp of Third World problems. After escorting her round a camp in Burkina Faso (then Upper Volta), West Africa, in February 1984, relief worker Abdullay Barry described how he'd found himself "grilled in minute detail by somebody who knew exactly what she was talking about. She wanted to know about the medicines dispensed, the training given to local staff, what problems we encountered, how we overcame them. She is totally involved." This month the Princess will be back in Africa, on a three-week tour of Tanzania, Mozambique, Zambia and Sudan.

The Save the Children Fund is more than delighted with its President. Says Director-General Nicholas Hinton: "Princess Anne not only works tirelessly on our behalf, but has always been quick to grasp that, despite frustrating local problems, we cannot always bang the table and demand that things be done quicker and better.

"If difficulties can be eased at an upper level, however, she has an unerring instinct for knowing how and which arms to twist." Fund staff noted, for example, how Princess Anne's 1981 visit speeded progress on several health projects in Nepal and Bangladesh.

**Whole-Hearted.** Princess Anne has always been quietly insistent that she be spared nothing in her efforts to see Fund work at grass-roots level. Never was this spirit more in evidence than on her 14,000-mile tour of seven African and Middle Eastern countries in 1982. For as *Daily Mail* reporter Stephen Lynas observed while covering the trip: "The Foreign Office have done everything they can to turn it into a safe, bland public relations exercise. The one person who has refused to let them is the Princess herself."

One major point of contention occurred over her projected visit to Beirut. With something close to civil war raging in the Lebanon, the Foreign Office was far from enthusiastic about the Princess visiting a Save the Children Fund team which was working from a cellar in the city, picking homeless children off the streets, dispensing food, drugs and equipment to the needy.

The battle over the visit raged back and forth. Only the day before she was due to fly from North Yemen did the Foreign Office give the go-ahead for her to stop off in Beirut.

"And was there any trouble?" I asked Princess Anne in a recent interview at Windsor Castle. "Just one or two bumps and bangs," she said casually. Close by? "It's always difficult to tell how close artillery fire is in a city," she shrugged—rather as if I had asked about the weather at a recent horse show.

The Princess has shown much the same intrepid calm since her earliest days. Born on August 15, 1950, Princess Anne Elizabeth Alice Louise enjoyed a happy but by no means spoilt childhood. A series of Scottish nannies helped inculcate the gritty frugality and thrift that is much in evidence to this day.

Prince Philip recognized in his lively, fair-haired daughter a spirit close to his own. By the age of six, she could dive from his shoulders into the swimming-pool at Buckingham Palace. At eight, seated on his lap, she learned to steer his Lagonda sports car on the private roads around Windsor Castle. He taught her to sail a dinghy on Loch Muick near Balmoral, to help crew his ocean-going yawl *Bloodhound* round the coast of Scotland.

**Proving Ground.** At Benenden, a boarding-school in Kent, she gained six GCE O level passes and A levels in history and geography. And soon after leaving school she became deeply involved in the equestrian sport of three-day eventing—a challenging combination of dressage, a long cross-country course and show-jumping. Princess Anne was doubly keen to excel since, as she put it, "It's the one thing the world can see that I can do well that has got *nothing* to do with my position, or money or anything else."

Inevitably, the Press regarded her riding, like everything she did, as potential news. Princess Anne thought differently. "Horses and eventing are part of my private life—that's outside working hours. If people choose to think that I'm going to behave in the same way at a highly competitive event, where the pace is fast and the hazards are testing, as I should and do behave at a public engagement, they expect too much."

The conflict with the Press led to occasional eruptions of royal fury. "On more than one occasion," recalls Princess Anne's trainer, Alison Oliver, "I suggested that she should go to the horse-box and stay there until she had cooled down."

The obverse side of this fiery temperament was the dashing verve of a superb horsewoman. In September 1971, less than three years after her first horse show, Princess Anne won the European individual three-day eventing championship. In 1972, she missed the chance of a team place in the Munich Olympics when her horse Doublet went lame; but in 1976, she did in fact become the first member of our royal family to compete in the Olympics when she was selected for the British team for the Montreal Games.

Meanwhile the world's Press had scented something else to fire its interest: romance. Another frequent eventing competitor and even more frequent winner was an officer in the Queen's Dragoon Guards, Mark Phillips. Just two years older than Princess Anne, he had already twice won the prestigious Badminton Three-Day Event, as well as a gold team medal at the 1972 Olympics.

**Evasive Actions.** To elude the Press, Princess Anne once travelled to meet the young captain in the back of a horse-box. On another occasion, she resorted to wearing a wig as a disguise when meeting him at an airport. "Nobody recognized me," she cheerfully recounts. "But then neither did Mark."

Finally, in May 1973, the engagement of the young couple was announced—to be followed by a story-book wedding in Westminster Abbey in November of that year.

Just four months later, the Princess and her husband were caught up in a nightmare ordeal. On the evening of March 20, 1974, they were being driven down the Mall on their way home from a London charity event. Suddenly a Ford Escort forced their car to a halt, and its driver appeared with a hand-gun [see "Seven Minutes in the Mall," RD, June 1975].

Trying to protect the Princess, her personal detective Inspector James Beaton was shot in the shoulder, the hand and the stomach before finally collapsing. Her would-be kidnapper —a schizophrenic later identified as Ian Ball—also shot her driver in the chest, then wounded a policeman and a passer-by who came to her help.

But as Ball repeatedly tried to drag her from her car, an ice-cool Princess Anne kept quietly talking to him, doing her best to distract his attention from the police who eventually over-powered him. So impressed was the Queen with her daughter's "calm and brave behaviour" that she appointed her a Dame Grand Cross of the Royal Victorian Order.

While royal security has since been tightened, Princess Anne is the first to recognize that "if somebody wants to kidnap me, and they really put their minds to it, they'll try to do it. But if you began to live with that thought always in your mind—well, you wouldn't move outside your front door."

Certainly, the Mall incident did nothing to restrict an increasingly hectic life. As well as bringing up two children—Peter, eight this month, and Zara, four—the Princess pitches in to help her husband farm Gatcombe Park's 1,200 acres.

"There's always a tractor to drive . . . bales to heave . . . animals to move," she explains. As the holder of a heavy goods vehicle driving licence—she drives horse-boxes—the Princess once surmised that, if need be, she could earn a living as a long-distance lorry driver.

Princess Anne has shown herself game for almost anything: taking part in a Radio 4 phone-in pro-gramme, writing an article for *Punch*. She is particularly will-ing to appear in what she considers a good charitable cause. Last April at Epsom, she sportingly donned royal racing colours to take part in her first-ever flat race. She finished fourth, helping to raise some £50,000 for the Riding for the Disabled Association.

Typically, as soon as she got her breath back, she declared, "The horse might have gone faster with someone else in the saddle. At no point did I think I could win."

But for thousands who lost money on their royal favourite that hardly mattered. As one punter happily ex-claimed, "Fourth place? Don't you believe it. In my book, Princess Anne is a winner every time."

PHOTOGRAPH: PAGE 108, JOHN SHELLEY

---

## Pension Plan

I WAS at a conference in London some years ago at which the principal speaker was Peter Walker, then Secretary of State for the newly created Department of the Environment. He told us there had been some difficulty in choosing a suitable name for the new Department and that various sugges-tions had been put forward, including "Department for Living."

"However," he went on, "if we had accepted that suggestion it would have made me Secretary of State for Life, and not even my own party would have worn that one." —A. Shepherd, Ickenham, Middlesex

# Windsor's Royal Pleasure Park

BY PETER BROWNE

**Come into the Queen's back garden—five thousand acres open for everyone to enjoy**

STROLLING through Windsor one fine afternoon, we stopped to admire the bay horse between the shafts of a handsome open carriage standing in the taxi rank beside the castle. "Hop in," said the bowler-hatted "taxi" driver, "and I'll take you to see the king."

*The king?* Intrigued, Joan and I clambered on board, to be driven down a side street and through an imposing iron gate. Gone was the tourist-jammed town: suddenly we were in the green expanse of Windsor Great Park and rolling on to the noble avenue of the Long Walk.

Northward it led back through Home Park to the state entrance of the castle—a right royal road, seen when television covers the arrival of the Queen's most eminent guests. Our humbler carriage turned south towards the Great Park, where the avenue stretches ruler-straight between rows of plane and chestnut to the foot of a distant hill. As we came nearer, overtaking hikers and joggers, we saw that it is crowned by a massive equestrian statue.

"There you are," smiled our driver. "King George III. His son, George IV, put it there as a tribute to 'the best of fathers.'"

Puffing on foot up steep Snow Hill, we stood beside the towering monument, known familiarly as the

*The majestic approach of the Long Walk; tranquil waters in Frogmore Gardens; the Copper Horse crowns Snow Hill; Valley Gardens ablaze with azaleas*

Copper Horse. The king, dressed as a Roman emperor, sits astride his mount surveying the vast panorama of wooded country below, with one hand raised as though inviting us to enjoy his domain. We accepted his offer on the spot. In the many times we have been back, we have come nowhere near exhausting the attractions of Windsor's royal parkland.

**Recreation Ground.** Home Park, 75 acres stretching from the Castle walls to the Thames, is the setting for spectacular summer events. In May we look forward to the four-day Royal Windsor Horse Show, offering everything from show-jumping to the Household Cavalry's splendid musical ride. Often we return to the same site in July for the Windsor Championship Dog Show, which attracts a whopping 10,000 entries. And Joan would never miss the summer Rose Show, which for more than 80 years has had the unique privilege of a place near the castle walls within "Home Park Private."

But our favourite haunt is the Great Park, whose delights we share with the royal family and around a million visitors a year. Not that you'd notice them. The place is so big—nearly 5,000 acres—that even on a Bank Holiday we have seen more deer than people, shared the solitude with fox and badger, heard only the tapping of woodpeckers.

In the Great Park, there's something for everyone. It's a fine place for flying model planes and kites, for the sponsored runs and walks which last year raised nearly £250,000 for charity, for quiet picnics under shady trees. You can roam afoot, on bike or horseback, fish its lakes, find a wealth of birds, animals and wild flowers. One afternoon last summer we met an ecstatic lepidopterist who had just spotted one of Britain's rare purple emperor butterflies.

The Great Park originated in the Middle Ages, when a park was simply enclosed hunting country. Fenced in by Edward I around 1278, it was known as the King's Park in the Forest of Windsor, and subject to stringent laws protecting game for "the chase." Ever since, Edward's successors have left their mark.

Within its 14-mile perimeter there are mighty oaks grown from acorns sown in 1580 by command of Elizabeth I, anxious to ensure future supplies for the Navy. The Long Walk was built for Charles II, "for his going out in diversion of Shooteing." Queen Anne laid down an avenue almost as long to take her from Windsor to the new race course on Ascot Heath.

**Grand Design.** It was George III and his uncle the Duke of Cumberland, appointed Ranger of the Great Park, who did most to shape it as it is today. They drained marshy land, put down plantations, built roads and model farms, and created Virginia Water, a huge artificial lake two miles long. "Farmer George" deserves his 25-foot-high statue—indeed it is said that before the horse was hoisted on to its granite base, 16 workmen climbed in to have lunch and drink the king's health.

For Queen Victoria, George's granddaughter, the Great Park was a treasured refuge from responsibilities: "Moroccan affairs very threatening," she wrote in her Journal, but the park "quite beautiful." She chose a peaceful spot in the gardens of Frogmore House near the castle for Prince Albert's domed mausoleum, and now lies there beside him.

The Queen often drove by carriage to Virginia Water. A state barge was kept on the lake for her, together with a miniature frigate which would sail past firing a 21-gun salute as she took tea on the shore.

**Idyllic Setting.** The lake itself covers 130 acres: a haunt of herons, Canada geese, and the brilliantly plumaged Mandarin ducks, for whom it is the major European habitat. It boasts a magnificent waterfall and, surprisingly, a cluster of Roman columns—brought from Leptis Magna in Libya around 1816, then planted by the waterside for George IV, living in the park at Royal Lodge, to "beautify his garden."

Today, the whole area at the park's south-east corner is a paradise for gardeners. Take the bridge across Virginia Water to the northern side, and you are in Valley Gardens, 400 acres of landscaped woodland carpeted in season with gorgeous azaleas, camellias and hydrangeas, and the greatest plantings of wild rhododendrons in the world.

Half a mile further on is the Savill Garden, surely one of the most delightful in the country, where some 90,000 people a year gladly pay to wander blissfully among glades ablaze with colour, from herbaceous borders to alpine plants and climbing roses. This is the home of rare magnolia species which are part of the Great Park's National Magnolia Collection, as well as of exotic plants, often unobtainable elsewhere, which you can buy. After our last visit, we carried home to our own suburban patch a brilliantly-coloured Himalayan poppy.

The 35-acre garden with its woods and streams looks like an exceptionally attractive piece of natural country. But it was created from a boggy wilderness, thanks largely to the enthusiasm of King George VI and Queen Elizabeth, who had adapted George IV's Royal Lodge near by as their country house, only 22 miles from Buckingham Palace.

Both were passionate gardeners, as was Eric Savill, Deputy Ranger of the park, who lived near by. "The King would come to inspect my roses, and I would go to look at his." They shared plants, and the royal couple became partners with Savill in planning the transformation of "the Bog Garden" into a superb public garden, finished in 1950 and named at the royal family's wish after Savill, who was later knighted.

It holds fond memories for the Queen Mother, who often comes over from Royal Lodge to slip through a discreet gate with her own key and enjoy the gorgeous rhododendrons in the Temperate House. The pink-washed Lodge has been a much-loved retreat for more than 50 years: her daughters spent much of their childhood there, and she describes it as a house that has known only happiness. To Prince Charles, a frequent visitor, it is "a haven of cosiness and charades."

In Charles's life, too, the Great Park plays an important part. From Royal Lodge it is only a mile or so through the woods to Smith's Lawn, an immense grassy stretch once used as a private airstrip by Edward Prince of Wales and now the site of a polo ground. The prospect of seeing Prince Charles in action in his favourite sport draws crowds to matches on summer weekends. Motives can be mixed. Joan once heard a breathless late arrival ask her friend: "Has he fallen off yet?"

The Queen herself enjoys a ride in the Great Park, though usually away from the public eye on royal farmland. Her pedigree Jerseys are exported as far as the Middle East and North America, and the herd provides the Castle and Buckingham Palace with cream, cheese and milk.

**Fair Deal.** The Queen pays rent for her 1,450 acres of farmland to the Crown Estate Commissioners, an arrangement which stems from George III's reorganization of the monarchy's finances some 200 years ago. He surrendered most of the royal lands—including Windsor Great Park, but not the Duchies of Cornwall and Lancaster—in exchange for an annual cash sum, the Civil List, intended to meet the expenses of the royal household. The lands, managed by the Estate Commissioners, last year provided a profit for the nation of nearly £18 million, after payment of a £5·18 million Civil List.

Prince Philip's ancient title of Ranger of the Great Park, conveyed on him by the Queen soon after her accession, is only honorary. Day-to-day management is in the hands of the Deputy Ranger, Roland Wiseman. Nevertheless he takes, according to Wiseman, "a great and active interest in all the park's affairs."

**Family Tradition.** George VI, Prince Philip's predecessor as Ranger, conceived the idea of The Village, not far from Royal Lodge, which he began building in 1949 to house some of the park's employees. Walk there from Ranger's Gate, and you'll find 60 attractive cottages surrounding the village green, with a combined post office and general store. The community centre, York Hall, is built of bricks salvaged from bombed sites in London. Altogether there are nearly 170 houses and cottages within the park, and 140 "pensioners' quarters" in pleasant purpose-designed buildings.

Many children brought up on the estate go to the Royal School, founded in 1845 by Queen Victoria, who instructed that "the School Mistress be furnished with a cow, milk being indispensable in the cooking department of the school." She also rebuilt the chapel in the grounds of Royal Lodge, where those who work and live in the park can join the royal family for Sunday worship.

The Deputy Ranger has a workforce of some 300 and an annual budget of just over £1 million to run Great Park, Home Park and the surrounding 7,600 acres of forest, where a large commercial sawmill produces an income of nearly a quarter of a million pounds a year. About 7,000 Christmas trees are cut every winter. The Queen gives a number to hospitals and children's homes; the rest are sold to add to income from car-parking and garden entrance fees which all help offset park costs. "We watch our expenditure closely," says Roland Wiseman, "but this isn't really a money-making enterprise. We are providing a service to the public."

**Support System.** Maintaining it is a formidable job. There are 25 miles of water mains, 530 gates, 125 miles of fencing which keep ten men permanently employed on repairs. Wiseman's staff includes the keepers of the six main gates in their gold-buttoned green uniforms, farm hands, park wardens, carpenters and builders, mechanics, foresters, game-keepers who look after the royal deer.

Close on 1,000 acres is the province of the red deer. The roaring of the stags sounds through woodland virtually unchanged since medieval days, when the oaks were pol-larded—the lower branches lopped and left lying so that in winter the deer could feed on the bark. When during the Second World War King George VI decided that a huge area should be ploughed to grow food, the herd was dispersed. But in Jubilee Year Prince Philip had much of the land returned to grass and brought in red deer from Balmoral.

Today a fence keeps the deer enclosed, but there are few restrictions on visitors to the park. By-laws prohibit such lapses as "behaving or being clothed in any manner reasonably likely to offend against public decency," and you need a £12 permit to try the three lakes for roach, eel and carp. Otherwise, you have the freedom of most of this five-by-three-mile stretch of unspoiled country.

In Windsor they fondly call it the Queen's back garden, and she uses the estate with an easy familiarity—visiting her mother, presenting prizes at the shows, enjoying a huge picnic to fund a cancer relief charity. She and Prince Philip have even been known to surprise castle guests with a personally conducted tour of the Great Park, taking it in turn to act as guides. After all, when they are at Windsor they are at home: the parkland an incomparable setting for what seventeenth century diarist Samuel Pepys described as "the most Romantique castle that is in the world."

PHOTOGRAPHS: ANDY WILLIAMS; PICTUREPOINT: J. ALLAN CASH

---

ANYTHING scarce is valuable, praise, for example. —Bits & Pieces

# They Fly the Queen

### BY PETER BROWNE

**Getting the royals there by air 800 times a year takes a unique body of men**

**L**ANDING precisely on time, the scarlet and white British Aerospace 146 jet rolled to a halt before the guard of honour at Kunming airport and the Queen was driven away to yet another round of official engagements. For the ten-strong RAF crew flying her on the 1986 tour of China there was still work to do.

By the time the Queen and her party boarded for take-off, the engineers had made a meticulous inspection of the royal aircaft. Everyone, including the pilots, had set to with buckets and sponges until not a speck of dust marred its immaculate finish.

Their Chinese hosts were astonished, but such perfectionism is routine for The Queen's Flight, a fleet of aircraft which operates to extraordinarily high standards. Whereas, for example, most airlines consider they are doing well if 98 per cent of their flights are no more than 15 minutes late, 99·95 per cent of royal flights arrive and depart within five *seconds* of schedule. Says the Duke of Edinburgh, "Such a record of reliability cannot be bettered by any commercial or military flying organization in the world."

Based at RAF Benson in Oxfordshire, The Queen's Flight—call

*Captain of The Queen's Flight John Severne (top left) on duty during the royal tour of China. Below: Wing Commander Mike Schofield, in charge of the men and machines. Ferrying the Princess of Wales to Wiltshire, Prince Charles to Glamorgan or the Princess Royal to North Yemen is all part of the service*

sign "Kittyhawk"—carries members of the royal family on more than 800 journeys a year. In overall command is John Severne, a genial retired air vice-marshal.

As Captain of The Queen's Flight, he accompanies the Queen and Queen Mother wherever they go by air, and is responsible for advising the royal family on all aspects of aviation, whether overseeing arrangements for the Duchess of York to earn her private pilot's licence or planning air journeys for a state visit overseas.

**Tour Operators.** Severne compares his role of Captain to that of a travel agent who deals directly with clients and makes their reservations, explaining: "Wing Commander Mike Schofield, the Commanding Officer of the Flight, actually runs the airline that takes them to their destination."

For Schofield, that involves managing a self-contained unit of five aircraft and 180 officers and men—all volunteers, and chosen from the RAF's best. The 11 pilots are expected to have an "above average" or "exceptional" rating and, for the captains, a minimum of 5,000 hours' flying experience. Ground crew must also be rated at least above average in the 15 trades, from carpenter to radio technician, needed to keep the royal fleet in A1 condition.

They are an élite group who receive no extra pay for royal service or overtime. Their professionalism is reflected in the closely guarded

Queen's Flight hangar at Benson, surely the only one anywhere with a polished floor, on which stand aircraft almost unbelievably pristine. Each has its glossy paintwork cleaned by some 50 men every week, the slightest blemish banished by a craftsman using a nail-varnish brush. Even the engines, hidden beneath their cowlings, are so scoured that they look brand new.

The fleet, all British, consists of two Wessex helicopters and three small airliners: a pair of BAe 146 four-engined jets acquired in 1986 for £32 million to replace elderly turbo-prop Andovers, and the remaining Andover, now 22 years old, which may eventually give way to a third BAe 146.

The aircraft earn their keep. Allocated to the royal family in order of seniority, they average between them around 70 flights a month within Britain and overseas. On a single day in June last year there were ten—ferrying the Queen and Prince Philip, the Prince and Princess of Wales and the Dukes of Kent and Gloucester to and from commitments in Scotland, Dorset, Norfolk and Lancashire.

The Queen's Flight carries visiting heads of state, among them recently President Mitterrand of France, King Hussein of Jordan, King Olav of Norway and the King and Queen of Spain. It can provide a fast response to disaster, like speeding the Prince and Princess of Wales to meet hospitalized victims of the Bradford football stadium

fire, or the Duke and Duchess of York to visit survivors from the capsized *Herald of Free Enterprise*.

It has also played a part in royal celebrations—a BAe 146 took the Duke and Duchess to the Azores on honeymoon, taxiing out at Heathrow with a JUST MARRIED notice attached to the air brakes. And it can assist at more sombre occasions, as when flying the Duchess of Windsor from France for the Duke's funeral.

The cost of it all? The annual bill for running the Flight, charged to the defence budget, is currently just under £5 million. As Air Vice-Marshal Severne points out, the RAF now has to spend £3 million to train a single Harrier pilot. "In that context, I think we represent good value for money."

Of all the royal aircraft, the most easily spotted are the Wessex helicopters in their vivid scarlet and blue livery. They enable the family to meet a programme which would have been impossible when take-offs and landings were confined to airports.

**Up and Away.** Prince Philip became the first to try a helicopter in 1953, taking off from the gardens of Buckingham Palace. Now the two Wessex collect their passengers from any of the eleven royal residences around the country and carry them virtually anywhere—even, on one occasion, delivering Prince Charles to the top of Snowdon to join a party of disabled climbers. Both Charles and his father have their personal pilots, who always fly with them, though they normally take the controls themselves.

A single day of royal visits within Britain can mean as many as nine different landing sites for the helicopters. Every one demands advance arrangements for security, medical cover and crowd control. The first time a Wessex flew Princess Diana, it was almost swamped by an eager crowd of some 3,000 on landing in a public park.

**Clear Course.** Safety is paramount. The helicopter route is chosen to avoid airfields and high ground, and for the duration of the royal flight it becomes a protected corridor of airspace, prohibited to all other military aircraft.

Wherever a royal Wessex lands, a crash-rescue and fire-fighting team must be on the spot. The Queen's Flight has its own support section: five multi-purpose trucks, their equipment including foam, hydraulic cutting gear, night-landing lights and a helicopter refuelling system.

The trucks are crewed by RAF firemen who organize the site before the helicopter arrives, liaising with local police. Then the men maintain radio contact with the pilot during his approach, advising him on weather conditions and the best landing direction.

Every aircraft of The Queen's Flight is kept 100 per cent serviceable. By tradition, the engineers work on any fault for 24 hours a day until it is put right. Last year Wing Commander Schofield returned in an Andover from the Middle East, having signalled ahead that there were signs of an oil leak around the hub of one propeller. After landing, the aircraft was towed into the hangar, and as usual no one was allowed off until after the customs check.

"While we were sitting in the Andover," remembers Schofield, "our engineers started work. Before we completed customs clearance, they had the propeller off and a new one in its place."

On long tours abroad, spares can be called up from anywhere in the world. During a recent royal visit to India, inspection of a BAe 146 at Delhi after landing on a Friday revealed that an engine bearing needed to be replaced. But the nearest source was the British Aerospace factory at Hatfield, Hertfordshire, and the next leg of the tour was due to be flown on Sunday.

**Team Effort.** When the signal reached Benson, Wing Commander Schofield had just four hours to complete hectic arrangements. A helicopter picked up the bearing from the factory, then flew it, with Queen's Flight engineers, to Heathrow. The engineers were met by a car which had collected their visas from the Indian High Commission in London. Arriving in Delhi after a nine-hour flight, the men worked on the engine through the remainder of Saturday—and got the plane ready in time for take-off.

It's all a far cry from the first official air journey by one of the royal family, in 1928, when the then Prince of Wales rode in an open-cockpit RAF Bristol fighter from Yorkshire to Norfolk. Becoming an aviation enthusiast, he soon had his own Gipsy Moth, and over the next few years bought a succession of private aircraft. All were flown by his personal pilot, Flight-Lieutenant Edward Fielden.

When the Prince became King Edward VIII in 1936, "Mouse" Fielden was appointed Captain of the newly formed King's Flight—with a single Dragon Rapide biplane, himself as sole pilot, two engineers and a secretary. Disbanded during the Second World War, the Flight reformed in 1946 with Fielden, now an air commodore, still in command. During the 16 years before he retired, his forceful personality shaped the Flight into the remarkable organization it is today.

**Bumpy Ride.** In Fielden's time the Flight was hardly a luxurious form of travel. The twin-engined Vikings used in the 1950s had armchair seats made notoriously uncomfortable by parachutes concealed in the upholstery.

The Herons which replaced them in the 1960s were so cramped there was no room for a galley. The only cooking possible was an egg boiled in a kettle. Their red fluorescent paint, designed to make them conspicuous, absorbed heat. In Ghana the Queen once had to endure a cabin temperature of 49 degrees C [120 F].

The Andovers which followed the Herons also had drawbacks. A maximum cruising altitude of 20,000 feet rendered them unable to climb above bad weather; storage space was no larger than a wardrobe, so that royal baggage overflowed into every corner, and the galley was little more than a cubby-hole.

**High Style.** Today's new BAe 146 jets, with their two-tone blue and grey interior colour scheme chosen by the Queen, are far more spacious and comfortable, flying 36 passengers nearly twice as fast at up to 30,000 feet, and with a much longer range of 1,600 miles. Both are equipped with big baggage holds and a magnificent galley from which stewards can conjure up a five-course meal.

The quietest of jets, BAe 146s have another great advantage for a royal family whose duties often take them to remote corners of the world: they can operate from smaller airfields than any other jet airliner. Largely because of their performance, more overseas tours have been scheduled for this year than ever before, covering more than 25 countries from Indonesia to Swaziland.

The planning of each overseas trip is done with typical Queen's Flight precision. At Benson the operations room has direct lines to airports throughout the world. Nearly every tour is preceded by a proving flight on which RAF aircrew and royal household officials check out everything from refuelling facilities to airport security—even such details as ensuring that when a BAe 146 taxis in, the red carpet will be unrolled to the rear door.

Notes Air Vice-Marshal Severne: "Because first-class commercial airline passengers alight at the front, it's hard to get through to people that the royal cabin is always at the back."

The proving flights can throw up unexpected snags—like the loose stones needing to be cleared from a primitive airstrip during the Princess Royal's 1985 tour of Africa, and the adjustable aircraft steps proudly offered by one airport manager for a royal arrival. Tested by a sceptical Queen's Flight engineer, the steps collapsed in a shower of hydraulic fluid.

**Mystery Trip.** China was an unknown quantity for Wing Commander Mike Schofield, who is the Queen's personal pilot as well as Commanding Officer of the Flight, when he flew a BAe 146 there in July last year on reconnaissance for the royal tour in October. While most countries publish full details of their civil airfields, air routes and radio beacons, China is reticent about all but its international routes. On the proving flight the BAe 146 had to carry a Chinese navigator and radio operator.

Often, only when it was airborne would they reveal any details of the out-of-the-way airfields they were heading for. "Neither of them spoke any English," recalls Schofield. "The navigator would point at a map and tell us through the interpreter: 'That's where we're going.'"

Like every royal tour, China involved The Queen's Flight in complex organization, with a multitude of timings to be calculated—down to the exact moment the aircraft door would open for the Queen on arrival at each stop. She travelled out in a chartered British Airways Tristar, and at Shanghai transferred to a Queen's Flight BAe 146 which had earlier completed a tour of the Far East with Prince Philip.

Wing Commander Schofield then flew the royal couple some 3,000 miles inside China and on to Canton, where they boarded *Britannia* and sailed to Hong Kong. From there the Queen returned to England by Tristar while the BAe 146 took Prince Philip back to China for a further tour before he in turn flew home.

Enough to baffle any travel agent, but for Air Vice-Marshal John Severne it was a familiar task and after four months of planning everything went without a hitch. Well, almost. Confesses the Captain of The Queen's Flight: "At Canton, the door was opened ten seconds late."

PHOTOGRAPHS: TIM GRAHAM; J.S. LIBRARY INT

---

### Read All About It!

WE USED to hiss the villain; now we go out and buy his book.

—Bill Copeland in Sarasota *Journal*

SPECIAL FEATURE

# ELIZABETH II
# Forty Years On

## BY TIM HEALD

S HE never forgets she is the Queen. For all her warmth and friendliness, this small, matter-of-fact woman remains at all times the anointed sovereign, a monarch caught in a web of romantic mysticism.

"You're always very aware exactly who she is," says Edward Mirzoeff, producer of the new BBC documentary about the Queen's working life, "Elizabeth R," being shown early this month to mark the fortieth anniversary of her accession to the throne.

TIM HEALD is the author of *The Duke: A Portrait of Prince Philip*, written with the co-operation of Buckingham Palace. A journalist since 1965, he has worked on *The Sunday Times* and *Observer*. Married with four children, he lives in Surrey.

"There's inevitably a certain remoteness about her. She never gives interviews, and you can't film her eating or drinking. Throughout our year of filming, I saw over and over again how all kinds of people are completely overwhelmed by her."

Mirzoeff, an award-winning television man more worldly wise than most, himself suffered the same experience when he was summoned to Buckingham Palace before filming began. Full briefings from two Palace officials, both concluding with admonitions not to be nervous, did little to allay his butterflies. Then, ushered in to meet the Queen for the first time, he was "bowled a googly" when the Queen was told that he would give a short exposition of how he envisaged the film.

"I hadn't even formed a plan of how to make the film, and I had no idea what to say," recalls Mirzoeff. "I felt as though I was gibbering and talking a load of codswallop. She was charming, but it gave me an insight into how terribly difficult it must be for her to cope with the effect she has on people."

But cope she does. To Elizabeth Alexandra Mary, being

The Queen at breakfast, painted by
HRH The Duke of Edinburgh; in conversation
with George Carey, Archbishop of Canterbury,
at Windsor Castle; work must go on even at
Balmoral—John Major flew to Scotland for an
audience with the Queen

Queen is much, much more than just a job. Her sense of duty and of service, consecrated by solemn oath and the anointing with holy oil at her Coronation service in 1953, is crucial to understanding Elizabeth II. Despite being in some ways the most unpretentious person, the Queen has a real sense of being called to fulfil an almost mystical task with a strong religious dimension.

Since she succeeded to the throne, Great Britain's place in the world has changed beyond recognition. Former colonies have become independent members of The Commonwealth, in which Britain is just one equal member — though the Queen remains entrenched as head of this disparate collection of countries, from Australia to Zambia. And every year sees the country's sovereignty further subsumed into the European Community.

Yet the Queen's sense of dedication remains as strong as it was almost 45 years ago when, on her twenty-first birthday, the then Princess Elizabeth broadcast to her future subjects: "My whole life, whether it be long or short, shall be devoted to your service and the service of our great Imperial Commonwealth to which we all belong."

## A Royal Day

THE Queen's life is not like other people's. Every morning she is serenaded by bagpipes — a tradition dating back to the reign of her great-great-grandmother, Queen Victoria. If you happen to be walking down Constitution Hill from Hyde Park Corner between 9 and about 9.15am on a day when she is at Buckingham Palace, you can hear the skirl of the pipes behind the high wall of the Palace garden.

It is an indication of the Queen's Scottishness as much as of her musical taste. On her paternal side that Scottishness is the ersatz "Balmorality" of Queen Victoria, who came to Scotland as a stranger, fell in love with the country and became almost more Scottish than the Scots. On her mother's side, however, it is very real. The Queen Mother, after all, is a Bowes-Lyon of Glamis Castle, a Scot to her fingertips.

Whenever possible, the Queen and the Duke of Edinburgh take breakfast together. In the Duke's private collection there is one charming oil he painted himself, which shows the Queen sitting at a table in their private dining room at Windsor Castle, a radio alongside a pot of marmalade on the white tablecloth.

Theirs is unlikely to be a silent breakfast. Although the press office prepares a summary of the day's newspapers so that the Queen can see at a glance what is going on in the world, the morning papers and radio news programmes are part of the breakfast routine. The Duke, a talkative and opinionated man, is accustomed to reading news items out loud and then subjecting them to pithy comment.

After 44 years of marriage and widely publicized rumours of "royal rifts" in earlier years, the Edinburghs, as they were once called, remain a close-knit team. They are often apart and habitually sleep in separate bedrooms but, as all those who observe them at close quarters tell you, they are the best of friends and it is impossible to imagine either of them taking a really important decision without consulting the other. "She is 500 per cent loyal to him," one former Palace courtier told me effusively, "and he to her."

Every morning there are papers to be worked on. The private secretaries' office sends up a box of documents ranging from suggestions for the appointment of bishops or ambassadors to requests for visits, speeches or openings. All are sorted, checked and minuted with comments and recommendations. At about 11 o'clock, unless the Queen has a public engagement, she usually sees one of her Private Secretaries.

The Private Secretaries are vital to the Queen, and the best of them become close and valued advisers and friends. In the whole of her reign the Queen has only employed six principal Private Secretaries. The first four were older than her, while the last two have been younger. Comments one expert: "An excellent thing." It has kept the Queen in touch with generations above and below her in age.

Since 1990 the principal Private Secretary has been Sir Robert Fellowes, a courtier's son and former banker who is married to Lady Jane Spencer, sister of the Princess of Wales. He is assisted by Sir Kenneth Scott, a career diplomat and former ambassador to Yugoslavia, and by vice-admiral's son Robin Janvrin, also formerly of the Foreign Office.

All three are urbane, charming, self-assured and comfortable in royal circles. Polite without being obsequious, efficient without seeming bureaucratic, they are very much the Queen's men. She likes men with whom she can feel at ease, and expects firm recommendations from them. Impatient with shilly-shallying and equivocation, she wants to know what people think.

Her husband and her eldest son maintain private "think-tanks" to advise them on the various subjects — the environment, architecture, equestrianism, technology — in which they like to stick an oar. The Queen, says one of her ex-advisers, "might have tried out a few thoughts on friends or relations, but there has never been anything like Prince Philip's little network of thinkers." The official view is that Her Majesty can call on her Ministers, her bishops, her generals and others whenever she wishes. A think-tank which bypassed the usual channels would be thought highly irregular, if not unconstitutional.

A typical day for the Queen includes much "kissing hands," a reminder of the ancient and solemn forms of court behaviour that are still maintained. Just after midday on June 4, 1991, for example, Robert Cormack, who had just been appointed

Her Majesty's Ambassador Extraordinary and Plenipotentiary at Stockholm "was received in audience by the Queen and kissed hands."

As he left Buckingham Palace at 12.40, the King of Swaziland arrived and stayed until almost 1pm. Immediately afterwards, the Queen received Major-General Sir Christopher Airy, who was "relinquishing his appointment as Private Secretary and Treasurer to the Prince and Princess of Wales." For each meeting the Queen will have been carefully briefed by one of her Private Secretaries.

Later that afternoon the Queen and the Duke of Edinburgh went to the Design Council in London's Haymarket to visit "A Hundred Years of British Invention," the centenary exhibition of the Chartered Institute of Patent Agents. By 6.30 she was back at the Palace in order to receive her Prime Minister and First Lord of the Treasury, John Major.

This weekly chat with the Prime Minister has taken place throughout her reign, though its contents are never divulged. At the time of the first, with Sir Winston Churchill, the present Prime Minister was a mere eight years old. Then it was Churchill who could call on a lifetime of experience to advise a novice. Today, with John Major 17 years the Queen's junior and a Member of Parliament only since 1979, the roles are reversed.

It is a totally private, one-to-one meeting. There are no secretaries or footmen present. Not even Prince Charles, who does see government papers and enjoys access to the Prime Minister and Cabinet whenever he wishes, sits in on these tête-à-têtes.

Relations with all nine Prime Ministers of the Queen's reign have been perfectly correct, though it is said that Her Majesty found Sir Anthony Eden difficult. Both her Labour Prime Ministers, Harold Wilson and James Callaghan, were bowled over by her. Says one old Palace hand: "Harold fell for her in a big way."

In contrast, the frostiness between her and Mrs Thatcher was a subject of widespread comment, public and private. "A model of propriety," says one man in a position to know. "Respect for all the conventions on Mrs Thatcher's hand, combined with an almost exaggerated degree of deference. And on the Queen's part, the acknowledgement that it is the Prime Minister's prerogative to govern, and the Sovereign's role to support her Government in fair weather and foul."

This extreme punctiliousness may well have disguised a certain instinctive mutual lack of empathy. The Queen finds it much easier to deal professionally with men. It is no coincidence that she has never had a female Private Secretary.

Sometimes in the evening the Queen and the Duke will go out together, though he is more of a night owl than she is. But often they perform official duties apart. On one typical day in 1991 the Duke had lunch at Trinity House and later dined with The British Heart Foundation at St James's Palace. The Queen was not involved in either of these occasions, any more than the Duke was at her various audiences.

When the Duke is out to dinner the Queen often eats alone in her private apartments, sometimes watching television, nearly always late. She drinks very little alcohol and follows a sensible, straightforward diet, though she avoids shellfish — as much a precaution against stomach upsets as a matter of taste.

Those solitary evening meals are sacrosanct. Even close family do not intrude without telephoning to arrange it first. "The royal family are all remarkably independent," says former Private Secretary Sir William Heseltine. It can make life difficult for the Palace officials. Individual members of the family have a disconcerting habit of not telling each other what they are up to. It is therefore imperative that the different households regularly compare notes. Otherwise they can find themselves in "awful messes."

For the Queen, the evening invariably brings more paperwork. As well as the afternoon box from the Private Secretaries, there are other government papers. When the House of Commons is in session, she receives a daily report on proceedings from the Vice-Chamberlain. Every year, too, the Queen receives thousands of letters — 49,023 in 1990 — from

members of the public. Each one is answered, usually by a lady-in-waiting or Private Secretary. The Palace rule is that "anything addressed to the Queen goes to the Queen's desk." So she always has plenty to read.

Being the sovereign is not a nine-to-five job, but the Queen's stamina is remarkable. She has never been known to complain about the tedium of long parades, banquets or state ceremonies.

Work and leisure are inextricably entwined. On one occasion in the 1960s, the Private Secretary of the day, Sir Michael Adeane, baulked at showing the Queen a memorandum prepared for her by a prominent public figure, saying it was too short on detail. On hearing of this the Lord Chamberlain, the altogether breezier Earl of Scarbrough, asked to see the memo. "Perfectly all right," he said. "I'll show it to Her Majesty myself."

Next day he called the author of the memo to say he had shown it to the Queen, who had approved it. "But when and where did you manage to do it?" asked the puzzled memo-writer.

The answer was simple. It had been the first day of the Royal Ascot race meeting when, before the first race, the Queen processes up the course in the state landau, accompanied by the Lord Chamberlain. Scarbrough had taken the controversial memo with him and produced it from the pocket of his morning suit as the procession set out. At the same time as he and the

## SPECIAL FEATURE

# ELIZABETH II
# Forty Years On

Queen smiled and waved at the crowd, they were discussing the document, kept well out of sight below the side of the carriage.

Even at parties, the Queen is not off-duty. At a Palace ball she was dancing with one of her bishops—as head of the Church of England, she always talks about "my bishops." "Tell me," she said as they waltzed round the floor, "what do you know about 'X'?"—the preferred candidate for a vacant bishopric, who was due to see the Queen next morning.

Later, still at the party, the bishop gave the Queen a considered confidential report on the man. "I really thought," he said later, "that she was going to get a pencil and paper there and then and write it down."

### Defender of the Faith

TIME and again when you talk to those who have worked closely with the Queen over the years, you are reminded: "She was anointed at her Coronation." For some, the symbolism of that Christian ceremony may be empty pageantry, but for her it represents an absolute truth. Noted Dermot Morrah, Arundel Herald Extraordinary—a member of the College of Arms whose ancient duties involve working on grants of coats of arms and helping to organize major state ceremonies: "The sense of spiritual exaltation that radiated from her was almost tangible to those of us who stood near her in the Abbey."

Since then, as one of her admirers puts it: "Her every decision is informed by her faith." The Right Reverend Robin Woods, who served her as Dean of Windsor and Domestic Chaplain from 1962 to 1970, describes her as "a praying and believing woman," and recalls one telling example of how seriously she takes her role as Head of the Church.

In 1966, the Church of England proposed an alternative prayer book, which had remained unchanged since the reign of James I, and the new version was sent for the Queen's signature. One night she telephoned Woods from Windsor Castle. "I don't think I should sign something which will change the liturgy," she said, "until we've at least prayed it through."

Since it was hardly appropriate to do this in a public service in St George's Chapel, the Dean agreed that first thing on Sunday morning he would conduct Holy Communion according to the proposed Alternative Prayer Book in his private Deanery chapel. And so, before breakfast, the Queen, Prince Philip and Princess Anne made their way from the Castle to the tiny chapel for the first "Family Communion" service according to the new rite. Only when they had "prayed it through" did the

Queen sign the order approving it.

Hers has always been a very conventional Anglican approach to religion—devout, but neither mystical like Prince Charles with his ideas inspired by Laurens van der Post, nor questioning like Prince Philip, who has published several slim volumes of theological debate. She attends church regularly, and takes her religious role very seriously; she was conspicuously upset by the failure of her sister's marriage to Lord Snowdon and her daughter's to Captain Mark Phillips.

Probably one of the most upsetting incidents of her entire reign, however, was Princess Margaret's ill-starred attachment to divorced Group Captain Peter Townsend. Public opinion was divided about whether the Queen's sister should be allowed to marry a divorced man, but such a marriage was clearly against the wishes of both the Church of England and the Government.

The Queen was, as always, unflinching in her awareness that in a conflict between personal happiness and doing what was "right," there could be only one answer. In 1955 Princess Margaret announced that, "mindful of the Church's teaching that Christian marriage is indissoluble, and conscious of my duty to the Commonwealth," she would not marry Townsend.

## Pomp and Circumstance

THE Queen's personal, private style is unostentatious almost to the point of austerity. But the public side of her monarchy, though in some respects less formal than in its early days, retains the grand trappings of majesty. This is very deliberate and conscious. She does not believe in a cut-price, bicycling monarchy.

Buckingham Palace, Windsor Castle and the great country estates of Balmoral and Sandringham continue to flourish, though Sandringham House was reduced by about 90 rooms during extensive refurbishment in 1974. There is the Queen's Flight with its scarlet Wessex helicopters and the new, specially adapted British Aerospace 146 jet-aircraft, and the custom-built royal trains, recently overhauled by British Rail. The Royal Mews still houses a host of state coaches, Rolls-Royces and other vehicles, including an ecologically sound electric-powered mini-van for the Duke of Edinburgh, who for years has been a passionate conservationist.

Perhaps grandest of all, there is the Royal Yacht *Britannia*, a 5,769-ton ocean-going liner. Since she was first commissioned in 1954, she has sailed more than 920,000 miles, showing the flag from the Arctic to the Antipodes. A Buckingham Palace of the waves, she has a dining hall big enough to accommodate a state banquet and a 26-strong Royal Marine band to impress foreigners.

On June 26, 1959, US President Dwight Eisenhower and Her Majesty Queen Elizabeth II, along with Canadian Prime Minister John Diefenbaker, opened the St Lawrence

Seaway, the great international canal which links the Great Lakes to the Atlantic Ocean. James Orr, then the Duke of Edinburgh's Private Secretary, was with the American party as they watched *Britannia* steaming majestically from Montreal towards Lake Ontario. After a few minutes, a bystander turned to Orr and said, in awestruck tones: "Thank God you haven't seen the President's yacht!" That vessel was a modest 64-foot cabin cruiser.

Completely refitted in 1987, *Britannia* has become a roving trade centre hosting a regular series of "Sea Days" which have generated millions of pounds worth of exports. During last year's royal visit to the United States, she was the scene of "Sea Day Symposiums" on behalf of British motor and aerospace manufacturers.

In a very real sense, *Britannia* still rules the waves, a symbol of the Royal Family's fundamental attitude to their role. Says Sir Hugh Casson, who helped with the yacht's interior design and has long associations with

the royals: "I think one thing the Royal Family have learnt from that amazing woman, the Queen Mother, is that if you are going to do something you should do it with style. She above all is a great one for royals being royal."

Certain fixed points in the royal calendar remain sacrosanct and immutable: Remembrance Sunday in November, when the Queen leads the nation in honouring its warrior dead by laying a wreath of poppies at the Cenotaph in London's Whitehall; the Royal Maundy Service on the Thursday before Easter, a traditional religious almsgiving to the poor, with purses of specially minted Maundy Money; Trooping the Colour on Horse Guards Parade to mark her official birthday in June, when she takes the salute from her Foot Guards and Household Cavalry; the State Opening of Parliament, when she reads a speech to members of both Houses, outlining her Government's intentions for the new session.

These great state occasions, at which the Queen effectively embodies the whole national spirit, are an opportunity to demonstrate that she is a vital part of the nation, dedicated to serving her subjects as much as reigning over

Coming home to Buckingham Palace after the State Opening of Parliament; a private sitting for the new royal portrait by Andrew Festing; with Polish President Lech Walesa at a state banquet held in his honour at Windsor Castle them. Throughout her reign they have remained the same in essence. Says Sir William Heseltine: "I am sure there was always a clear idea in the Queen's mind of the proper way for her to conduct herself as head of state. The role is pretty well defined for her."

The years have brought some minor changes, however. The Royal Maundy service always used to take place at Westminster Abbey. Now it moves to a different cathedral each year—an innovation suggested by the Queen, who from the beginning has felt it important to be seen by people outside the capital and the favoured south-east of England.

At her Birthday Parade, she used until recently to ride side-saddle in a splendid scarlet and dark blue uniform with a tricorn hat. This Guards uniform is her only uniform—unlike the male members of her family, who have different ones for each of the services or regiments with which they are associated. It was, however, discreetly altered every year so that the jacket buttons and hat plume were those of whichever regiment's colours were being trooped.

It was only when her favourite steed, Burmese, grew too old that she switched to wearing "civilian" clothes and travelling by carriage to Horse Guards Parade. The decision had nothing—apparently—to do with the alarming occasion on June 13, 1981, when a 17-year-old youth fired some blank cartridges from a replica pistol at the Queen as she rode in procession down the Mall.

Part of the routine of monarchy is entertaining foreign heads of state. There are normally two state visits a year; when President Mubarak of Egypt came last July, it was the sixty-sixth state visit of the reign.

Other heads of state call on a less formal basis. Last year they included the presidents of Bulgaria, Chile, Hungary, Malawi and the USSR—then still in full-blown existence. These visits require less pomp and circumstance—no flags in the Mall, no state banquet or horse-drawn procession—but still the necessity, for the Queen, of ensuring she is at least well enough briefed to engage her guest in informed conversation. Critics who suggest she never reads a book, not even from the holiday reading submitted every summer by the Book Trust, fail to consider the prodigious quantity of papers she has to plough through in order to give a consistent impression of being thoroughly well informed.

In addition, the Queen is an indefatigable traveller. Soon after her Coronation in 1953, she toured the Commonwealth, visiting ten countries from Bermuda to Uganda. In her Jubilee Year, 1977, she and the Duke of Edinburgh covered an estimated 56,000 miles. Her first state visit, in 1955, was to Norway; her most recent, last October, was to Zimbabwe for the Commonwealth Conference.

She has always attached almost as

much significance to her role as head of the Commonwealth as she has to her position as Queen of the United Kingdom. But while she and her husband enormously value their links with the Commonwealth, they are both quite clear that they will only maintain them as long as people want them.

Both Australia or Canada have, in some quarters at least, exhibited an irritation with monarchy. The largely francophone Canadian province of Quebec is almost the only part of the Commonwealth where she has not been received with popular enthusiasm; during her 1964 visit there were even serious assassination threats. If republican feeling gets out of hand in either country, then the Queen will withdraw gracefully.

She is as well briefed on her Commonwealth countries as on Britain itself. After all, she has had a regular first-hand acquaintance with many of them for more than 40 years of her reign; for instance, she first visited Canada in 1951. And she understands why Canada is unique. "To become a Canadian citizen," she once said, "implies a commitment to share the particular gifts of personality and culture, which the newcomer brings with him, with the rest of the family of Canadians." If the frequency of her visits is an indicator, Canada is one of her favourite destinations. She has been there 17 times as Queen, compared to 11 visits to Australia.

At every Commonwealth Heads of Government Meeting, she receives each country's delegate for a 20-minute audience. She relishes the opportunity to see old friends, as well as forging fresh relationships with newly elected prime ministers. They, in their turn, "adore her," as one courtier says with both admiration and astonishment.

## Royal Riches

RUNNING a stylish monarchy does not come cheap. The 1990 estimate for royal garden parties, for instance, was £213,650; for flowers, £37,950; and for the upkeep of horses and carriages, £149,025. The Royal Yacht cost the taxpayer more than £9 million, the Queen's Flight almost £7 million and the Royal Train just over £2 million.

It would of course be possible to cut back on these, but if you did, say royalty's defenders, you would have a cut-price monarchy like the Swedes or the Danes. It is partly because the British royal family conducts its affairs with such style that the Queen is, for example, invited to address both houses of Congress or accorded the privilege of a White House state banquet.

Yet the question of the royal finances has been an irritant throughout the reign. Critics resent the fact that the Queen is alleged to be the richest woman in the world, and take particular exception to the fact that she pays no tax. As Willie Hamilton, then Labour MP for West Fife, wrote in 1969: "In the context of millions of our people existing on less than £10 a week, and at least half a million children suffering the direst poverty, the crown seems to many to be a vulgar extravagance."

After four decades of this sort of criticism, the Royal Family and their advisers respond with increasing weariness. So much of their presumed wealth, from the great art collection to the Crown Jewels and the palaces themselves, is not disposable but is kept in trust for the nation. "After all," said the Queen Mother to me once, "it's not as if one could buy a hat with Hampton Court."

On tax, three separate issues can be identified. The first is that at the beginning of her reign, the Queen surrendered the Crown Estates to the Government in return for a Civil List to cover the Crown's expenses, 70 per cent of them wages and salaries. In 1990 this Civil List was set at an annual £7·9 million (with adjustments for inflation) for a ten-year period.

The royal servants paid from the Civil List are taxed just like everyone else. Therefore, runs the argument, taxing the Civil List at source would mean submitting it to double taxation. You might just as well ask individual ministries to pay tax on their annual budgets. Incidentally, the Queen's Civil List is less than the money allotted to the Prime Minister's office every year.

The second major source of income is the revenue from the Duchy of Lancaster, supervised by the Chancellor of the Duchy—currently Tory party chairman Chris Patten. In the year ended on September 29, 1990, the total Duchy income was £4,088,767, of which £3 million was paid to the Privy Purse.

This money is used to cover "the sovereign's personal expenses," including the maintenance of Balmoral and Sandringham; to pay junior royal family members for any royal duties they perform; and to reimburse the Civil List for the allowance made to Princess Alexandra, the Duke of Kent and the Duke of Gloucester.

While the money could in theory be taxed, such a high proportion of it—possibly as much as £1 million a year—goes to maintaining Balmoral Castle that, say royal advisers, taxation would make it impossible to keep the castle in the royal family. This, it is presumed, would be very unpopular in Scotland.

Third, there is the Queen's personal income, which is undisclosed as well as being untaxed. Last March, Buckingham Palace was stung when *Harpers & Queen* magazine alleged that the Queen's personal wealth was £6·6 billion, yielding £1·8 million a day. Lord Wyatt sprang to Her Majesty's defence. He quoted the evidence of Lord Cobbold, a former Governor of the Bank of England who, as Lord Chamberlain, told a House of Commons committee in 1971: "Her

Majesty has been much concerned by the astronomical figures which have been bandied about . . . suggesting that the value of these funds may now run into £50 million to £100 million . . . She wishes me to assure the committee that these suggestions are wildly exaggerated."

Wyatt suggests the figure was more likely to have been £20 million and that, however well invested, this would now be worth no more than £120 million, yielding about £6 million a year in income.

The same magazine article also suggested that the Queen owns property worth £3 billion in Europe and North America. Palace officials say quite categorically that the Queen does not own "a single centimetre" of land outside the United Kingdom.

Most of the Queen's "wealth," according to the Palace, generates no income. There is no revenue from jewellery or pictures, excluding the Queen's Gallery where takings are devoted entirely to maintenance.

This leaves the riches the Queen inherited from her father. King George VI was not, protest his descendants, as rich as is supposed, largely because he had to buy Balmoral and Sandringham from his brother Edward VIII, who needed the cash to finance his very comfortable exile after his abdication. More recently, George VI's fortune has been used to support his widow, the Queen Mother, and younger daughter, Princess Margaret.

The Queen banks at Coutts and is always said not to carry money, although in the last royal film it did *look* as if she was shopping with her own petty cash. If money is ever needed, her lady-in-waiting will usually handle it.

If anyone doubts that the royal fortune is much exaggerated, they should consider how the Queen is cutting back on her racing interests. Early last year she had 35 flat-racers in training; by 1993 the number will probably be down to 25. In 1990, according to her racing manager, the Earl of Carnarvon, the Queen's horses won £212,000 in prize money.

But, says Lord Wyatt, who as Chairman of the Horserace Totalisator Board since 1976 is presumably in a position to judge: "With apologies to Her Majesty, I suspect she makes substantial losses at racing."

It would, nevertheless, be perfectly possible for the Queen to pay tax on her private income, although to do so would court all sorts of problems. The royal investment portfolio would be subject to relentless scrutiny. If it revealed that, for example, she had shares in foreign arms or tobacco companies, her opponents would have a field day.

While Her Majesty is not financially accountable in the way her subjects are, monarchists insist that the whole essence of the institution is that an element of mystery should be preserved. Start hacking away at that mystery, and you run the risk of damaging the monarchy beyond repair.

## In the Beginning

IN FEBRUARY 1952, when Elizabeth became Queen, it took three and a half days to fly to Sydney—most people went by boat still. A new Austin A40 "Somerset" car cost £467, with an extra £260 in purchase tax. The hot new film was *Quo Vadis*, an epic drama set in the reign of the Roman emperor Nero. There were anti-British riots in Cairo, a cockatoo called Old Bill celebrated his hundredth birthday at London Zoo, and comedian Jimmy Edwards was elected Rector of Aberdeen University.

In this half-forgotten yesterday's world, the young Princess Elizabeth and the Duke of Edinburgh flew out of London Airport on January 31 to undertake a tour of Kenya, Ceylon and "The Great Dominion" of Australia. In the photographs of the airport farewell, King George VI looks gaunt and painfully ill. A heavy smoker, he had had a lung removed the previous September because of cancer. But Mike Parker, the young Australian who was Equerry-in-Waiting to their Royal Highnesses, says that to those actually present the King seemed buoyant and well. "Otherwise we wouldn't have gone," he says. "It's as simple as that."

A week later the King was dead. It took some time to contact the remote Sagana Lodge in Kenya, where the new Queen and her consort were sleeping after a night watching wild animals from the nearby Treetops Hotel, but eventually Parker was officially informed of the King's death. He woke the Duke, told him the news and left him to tell his wife. Philip, he recalls, was deeply shocked, looking as if the world had dropped on his shoulders.

Hours later on that fateful February 6, after a logistic scramble to find suitable aeroplanes and rearrange their plans, the royal party left for London Airport. The Queen, "pale and regal," was a sad-eyed lonely figure as she came down the aircraft steps to be greeted by her prime minister, Winston Churchill, and her leader of the opposition, Clement Attlee, both wearing the black top hats convention required.

The King was dead. Long live the Queen. The next day the heralds at St James's Palace, in

At the Cenotaph on Remembrance Sunday, November 11, 1990; the family firm—with Charles and Diana on the occasion of the Queen Mother's birthday, August 4, 1987, and at Trooping the Colour with the Queen Mother and Princess Margaret

Whitehall, at Temple Bar and at the Royal Exchange read out the solemn proclamation of her accession. The second Elizabethan Age had begun.

For a few years there was a honeymoon period with the public; the Coronation in June 1953 touched powerful chords. But the early years were not always easy.

The royal couple were young and inexperienced, as they themselves are now the first to admit. Until recently they had spent time as an almost normal naval couple in Malta, where Prince Philip commanded HMS *Magpie*, a frigate in the Mediterranean Fleet. Had the king survived, Prince Philip, a highly proficient officer, could have continued to serve and, says his contemporary, Admiral of the Fleet Lord Lewin, would have risen to the top. It is one of the few regrets to which Philip now admits.

The Queen was still only in her mid-twenties and until her marriage in 1947 had spent her whole life at home with her family, educated by nannies and governesses. But, as so often with the monarchy, appearances were deceptive. "She was always very grown-up for her age," says Lord Charteris, her Private Secretary from 1950 to 1977, "very mature and very strong."

In no way did she seem overwhelmed by the role she had inherited. "She was a shy girl to begin with," says one former courtier and ardent admirer. "But she soon managed to use her charm and, dare I say it, sexuality, to win over the most unlikely people."

In addition, she unquestionably drew strength from her indomitable mother and her charismatic and resolute husband.

Her children, Charles and Anne, were only three and a half and 18 months old. She had just set up the first real home of her own, at Clarence House, now the home of the Queen Mother. To have to leave these newly decorated, comfortable surroundings for the bleak office block that is Buckingham Palace was a blow.

The Duke of Edinburgh even suggested to Churchill that as the two buildings were only a few hundred yards apart, the royal couple could go on living at Clarence House and merely treat the Palace as an office. But Churchill was having none of it and slapped Philip down quite brusquely.

Survivors of this era agree that while Churchill doted on the young Queen, he was less sure about her progressive husband. Philip was determined, in his own words, "to adapt to changing attitudes." Somehow the monarchy had to "feel our way into appropriate circumstances." One favourite example is the abolition of the old court presentations for debutantes, regarded as an integral and crucial part of their "coming out" season.

Instead, the Queen and her husband transformed the Palace garden parties so that now, three times a year, as many as 8,000 people converge on the lawns behind Buckingham Palace for tea or iced coffee, sandwiches and a chance of meeting or at least spotting a member of the Royal Family. One concession, however, remains to the old presentations: guests are allowed to bring along their unmarried daughters over the age of 18.

It is difficult now to tell how far the modernization of the monarchy was an independent initiative and how far a response to outside pressures. But in 1957, shortly before the presentations were abolished, the honeymoon between crown and people ceased abruptly when a widely quoted magazine article by old Etonian peer Lord Altrincham attacked many aspects of the royal family.

Among his criticisms, Altrincham maintained that the royal family's entourage was "tweedy." This still rankles, but even today it is not altogether unjust. "People sometimes feel there are an awful lot of retired admirals and generals around the Crown," says Sir Hugh Casson. "But at least they always turn up on time!"

The Coronation had induced a mood which was superficial and impermanent, said Altrincham, who disclaimed his title in 1963 to become plain John Grigg. Later, he described the ceremony as "an interlude of solemn pretence, an orgy of make-believe, in which the mass media were in league with the most blindly conservative forces in our

society." What caused the greatest uproar—and obscured more serious points he was making—was Altrincham's criticism of the Queen's speeches. Subsequently he explained that when he described the Queen's speaking style as a "pain in the neck," he meant only that she should strive for a greater degree of spontaneity. He also said that his references to "a priggish schoolgirl, captain of the hockey team, a prefect, and a recent candidate for Confirmation" did not mean that Her Majesty *was* any of these things, only that she sounded like it because "her real character was being hidden behind a mask of synthetic regality and sacerdotal pomposity."

The row was enormous. Altrincham received more than 2,000 letters of protest in the first week, was slapped in the face by a member of the League of Empire Loyalists, and was challenged to a duel by an Italian monarchist.

Before long, however, it became clear that the outrage was not universal. The *Daily Mirror* reported that its postbag was running four to one in favour of Altrincham's strictures. The *Daily Mail* published a National Opinion Poll which showed 35 per cent of those questioned were in general support of Altrincham, with 52 per cent against. Significantly, among the Queen and Prince Philip's contemporaries in the 16 to 34 age group, the figures were almost reversed, with 47 per cent for Altrincham and 39 against. Today, some of those close to the Royal Family agree that he did the monarchy a service.

The royal honeymoon was over in another sense, too. Back in 1948 there had been a Press story about the Duke of Edinburgh and the actress Pat Kirkwood, at the time the girlfriend of the society photographer Baron, who had been observed dancing together in a London nightclub in the small hours. In fact Baron was present, as was an upright naval officer called Captain "Basher" Watkin. Nothing improper occurred, but it set tongues wagging.

Then in 1956 the Duke embarked on a lengthy world cruise in the Royal Yacht, showing the flag in the remotest parts of the Commonwealth. It was an entirely proper thing for him to do, but it meant he was away for the state opening of Parliament, and that the royal couple were apart at Christmas. "Royal rift" became a murmur in the popular press.

In February 1957, the couple were reunited at Lisbon for a state visit to Portugal. During the tour the Duke had grown a much-photographed ginger beard. When he entered the aircraft which had brought his wife to Lisbon, he was disconcerted to find that every single person on board, from the Queen to the most junior member of the Household, was wearing a false beard. The Queen's sense of humour and fun, honed over many years of after-dinner charades, had produced a perfect practical joke. When the couple emerged to face the photographers, they presented not only a united but a laughing front—an excellent riposte to rumour.

In those days the "Family Firm," as George VI used to call it, was a very small unit. For the first 15 years of the reign the only mature adults capable of undertaking royal duties were the Queen and Prince Philip, the Queen Mother, Princess Margaret, the then Princess Royal (Mary), the Duchess of Kent (Princess Marina) and the Duke and Duchess of Gloucester. The core of the royal family was what Michael Mann, former Dean of Windsor, refers to as "the inner circle": the Queen Mother and her daughters, strong-willed characters all. As royal watchers put it, "If you crossed one, you crossed them all."

They were, and remain, very close to each other. "I always find it very affecting at Royal Lodge, after church on Sundays, to see how solicitous the Queen Mother is about the Queen," says one acquaintance. "Frightfully anxious to see that she has her favourite drink, mixed just right, and all that kind of thing."

By the late 1960s, however, the situation of the Royal Family had changed. Late blooming parentage had come to the Queen with the birth of Prince Andrew in 1960, a decade after his sister Anne, and Prince Edward in 1964. On the family fringe the young Kents, notably the Duke and Princess Alexandra, had grown up and were able to take some of the strain off their elders.

More important, Prince Charles was coming of age, an event marked

# ELIZABETH II
## Forty Years On

**Our exclusive, revealing portrait
of a Queen and her reign**

By Tim Heald

by his Investiture at Caernarfon Castle. It was the most spectacular royal jamboree since the Coronation, unashamedly geared to the needs of Press and television, a lavish piece of pageantry which signalled his emergence as a public figure in his own right.

Not only was there a huge media circus to coincide with the Investiture, there was also a special television film. This, for the first time, went behind the scenes at Buckingham Palace and Balmoral to show the royals as real people, enjoying a family barbecue (Prince Philip is particularly proud of his skills over the charcoal), shopping in Ballater, rewarding the horses with sugar and carrots.

Five years earlier, such revelations would have been unthinkable. That inveterate but constructive critic John Grigg believed the film had a great effect on the Queen herself. Looking back in 1970, he wrote: "The universal appreciation shown for the Queen's natural self, at last revealed, must have proved to her that the magic of her office did not depend on mystification, but was at its most potent when allied to spontaneity and truth. There is already evidence that she is more confident . . . and more willing, as it were, to depart from her script. In Australia this year [1970] she was unprecedentedly relaxed in crowds, initiating the practice of walking among them casually." Since then, of course, the royal walkabout has become commonplace.

Much of the initiative for the film came from the newly appointed Press Secretary, Bill Heseltine, a breezy Australian who has been one of the most influential courtiers of the reign. John Grigg attributes his success to the fact that he was so unlike the conventional Palace official. "But unfortunately one has to regard it as a one-off," he adds, "since the Household hasn't evolved to the point of being remotely representative of the Commonwealth as a whole. In particular, there are still no brown or black or yellow faces in it, which is surely quite wrong."

### Behind the Mask

"IF ASKED what I thought about the Queen," says James Orr, former private secretary to Prince Philip, "my immediate answer would be that she is a thoroughly human, natural person who puts her country, her family, her Household and friends before herself." Bill Heseltine, who retired in 1990 and now lives in Australia, refers to her as "that most straightforward of persons, my former boss."

Behind the often austere, unsmiling public image lies an amusing, relaxed private one. Someone on the fringes of the royal circle told me how at Windsor one afternoon a page came into the drawing room and said that there was a telephone call for the Queen. Her Majesty excused herself and left the room, only to return seconds later. "Sorry," she said, smiling. "Wrong Queen!"

She *can* laugh at herself—it's just

*The Queen greets the crowd at Hobart, Tasmania in 1970*

that she doesn't think it's always a proper thing for the monarch to do. At a 1972 luncheon in London's Guildhall to mark her Silver Wedding, she lightheartedly recognized what had become a national joke when she started her speech: "I think that everyone will concede that today, of all occasions, I should begin my speech with 'My husband and I.'"

Robin Woods remembers how the ice gradually seemed to break after he moved into the Windsor Deanery in 1962. His young family were very much of an age with the Queen's own children, which helped to break down barriers. But for three years, whenever he was received by the Queen he always changed into his formal Dean's garb of frock coat and gaiters. Then one Saturday while he was gardening, the Queen's page telephoned to say that Her Majesty wished to see him as soon as was convenient. The Dean replied that he must change first. The page repeated his message, the Dean insisted. Finally the page went off to consult his mistress and came back with an order that the Dean was to come at once, and was not to bother with what he was wearing.

When he arrived, he found his sovereign still in her jodhpurs after riding. From then on, the Dean never dressed up for such informal encounters. Although the matter was never mentioned, he felt it represented a definite thaw in their relations.

In private or semi-private, the Queen can be exceedingly relaxed about dress. On one occasion when reviewing the Fleet from *Britannia*, she was in ceremonial kit above the waist but below it, visible only to members of her immediate entourage, she wore sensible warm trousers to protect her from the brisk breezes of the English Channel.

This relaxed monarch is one the public rarely if ever glimpses. "I spent much of my time trying to let the public see the Queen that I knew and loved," says one faithful old servant wistfully. "I'm not sure I really succeeded. She's a much

It's not all work, work, work . . .
The Queen enjoying a ride at
Sandringham; the race-goer who
likes a flutter, Derby Day, June
1989; a monarch's best
friends—the royal corgis

nicer, funnier person than is often realized. And she has this golden honesty."

One day recently, she and half a dozen friends were picnicking in a secluded corner of the Balmoral estate. Traditional Scottish rights of access mean that, as one member of the little party remarked, "there is nothing very private about private property in Scotland." And as the royal group were "lolling about replete after a delicious picnic," a group of hikers marched past.

Suddenly the boldest of them turned back and confronted Her Majesty. "They say you're the Queen."

"Yes," she replied. "So I am."

"What are you doing here, then?" asked the hiker.

"I live here," the Queen said simply.

Her friends were taken aback by the confrontation. But not the Queen. Says one of the party: "Her response was unforced and precise, without artifice or prevarication. And that is her most notable characteristic—a dazzling truthfulness and unpretentiousness."

Richard Crossman, when Lord President of the Council, was critical of the apparatus and formality of royal life but, like so many others, was personally impressed by the Queen. "She laughs with her whole face," he wrote, "and she just can't assume a mere smile because she's really a very spontaneous person."

Unfortunately, as Crossman put it, "When she is deeply moved and tries

to control it, she looks like an angry thundercloud. So, very often when she's been deeply touched by the plaudits of the crowd, she merely looks terribly bad-tempered."

Sir Edward Bridges, who was Permanent Secretary to the Treasury during the first years of the Queen's reign, recalled one Privy Council meeting when four Privy Councillors, kneeling loyally before their monarch, became confused and scurried hither and yon on their knees. They knocked a book off a table, which the Queen caught. She looked bleakly furious. Afterwards Sir Edward apologized for the chaos. "You know," replied the Queen, "I nearly laughed."

The problem is that she always has to be wary about maintaining a distance between herself and her subjects, however intimate they may be. Sir Hugh Casson recalls an encounter at Windsor Castle when he was summoned to advise on some aspect of refurbishment.

The Queen came into the room wearing a particularly fetching outfit. Sir Hugh complimented her on it and then, without thinking, found himself grasping the lapel of the Queen's jacket between finger and thumb. He knew, as he did it, that he had overstepped the mark. Nothing was said. "But," says Sir Hugh, "I could feel the tinkling of ice."

In a very English way, these demarcations are never formally laid out. "No one ever tells you anything," says one old hand. You are expected to learn the rules by a mysterious process of osmosis.

One Balmoral guest told me how he had been present at a small house party. After tea the company adjourned to the drawing room and the Queen went to a card table and began to play patience. The guest was faced with a dilemma: sit too far away from the monarch and he would seem stand-offish, sit too close and he would look presumptuous.

Choosing a chair which seemed to be an appropriate compromise he sat down, and was soon aware that the Queen was looking at him. Presently she beckoned him over and proceeded to explain the rules of patience.

That evening, before dinner, the Private Secretary spoke to the guest. "That chair you were sitting on this afternoon was Queen Victoria's favourite," he said. "No one else sits on it."

The private secretaries and other members of the royal staff are as close to the Queen as all but the closest family and friends. Even "Crawfie," the one-time governess Marion Crawford who sold out by becoming one of the first purveyors of royal slush-and-gossip, was nevertheless a seminal influence on the young Princess.

An even greater and more enduring influence was Margaret "Bobo" Macdonald, who joined the family as an under-nurse when Elizabeth was still in her infancy, became her "dresser" and still in retirement—she was born

## Quotable Quotes

MAN is a gregarious animal, and much more so in his mind than in his body. He may like to go alone for a walk, but he hates to stand alone in his opinions.
—George Santayana

THE IMPROBABLE happens just often enough to make life either disturbing or delightful.
—William Feather

I ALWAYS like to hear a man talk about himself, because then I never hear anything but good.
—Will Rogers

THE WORLD is round so that friendship may circle it.
—Pierre Teilhard de Chardin

ONE THING in favour of real life —it takes your mind off all that suffering on television.
—Kelly Fordyce

IF I DO NOT believe as you believe, it proves that you do not believe as I believe, and this is all that it proves.          —Thomas Paine

HUMAN beings are perhaps never more frightening than when they are convinced beyond doubt that they are right.—Laurens van der Post, *The Lost World of the Kalahari* (Hogarth)

TOO much rest is rust.
—Sir Walter Scott

in 1904—retains a private apartment in Buckingham Palace. Douglas Keay, the latest and one of the best informed of royal biographers, claims that she enjoys "a closer personal friendship with the Queen than practically anyone else" and "is held in awe by even the most senior members of the Queen's Household."

Lord Carnarvon is an old and valued friend. So is Lady Susan Hussey, wife of Marmaduke Hussey, chairman of the BBC governors, who has been Lady of the Bedchamber—a sort of senior lady-in-waiting—since 1960. When Prince William of Wales was born in 1982, Lady Hussey was asked to be godmother, an exceptional honour for a lady-in-waiting.

The Duke of Edinburgh's private secretary Lord Rupert Nevill, who died prematurely in 1982 while still in office, was a genuinely close friend of both the Queen and the Duke, and his widow remains a valued confidante. There are other shadowy figures who come to stay and who are unknown even to close observers. "There was that man who always came to Windsor at Christmas," they will say mysteriously.

At such family gatherings, of course, there are also her six grandchildren, ranging in age from the Princess Royal's son Peter Phillips, who is 14, to the nearly two-year-old Princess Eugenie of York. The Queen seems genuinely fond of them but, unlike her demonstrative daughters-in-law the Princess of Wales and the Duchess of York, she is never seen cuddling or hugging them.

Given the inevitable isolation of her position, it is hardly surprising that the Queen sometimes seems to prefer the company of animals. All her life she has been close to dogs and horses. Once during a transatlantic flight the Duke, an accomplished pilot, went forward to inspect the flight deck. Afterwards, the flight captain asked if Her Majesty would like to do the same. The Duke, so the story goes, replied, "Certainly not. If it doesn't have four legs and eat grass, she's not interested."

Throughout her reign she has been an enthusiastic racehorse owner, who would be thrilled to win the Derby, the only one of the five English classics that still eludes her. She loves riding—without a protective hat—which also helps her to keep fit. And she probably knows as much about the family trees of horses as she does about those of people. "She's immensely knowledgeable on pedigree," says Lord Carnarvon, "and a very good judge of an animal. In fact, I'd say breeding interests her more than racing. For her it's a wonderful means of switching off from state duties."

Her corgis, dorgis (corgi-dachshunds) and Labradors are an even more passionate interest. At many informal occasions the corgis are present, sometimes all seven of them—Phoenix and Pharos, Fable and Myth, Spark and Diamond, and Kelpie. Not only does the Queen like them for their unquestioning loyalty, they also serve as ice-breakers, a useful topic of conversation at difficult moments. When the Queen starts to show impatience by playing fretfully with the rings on her wedding finger or tapping a toe on the carpet, a comment on corgis may come in useful.

On one famous occasion she was quite badly bitten when trying to separate rival packs of her corgis. She has also been known to appear in company looking distinctly muddy after trying to coax the royal dorgis out of the earth when they went to ground. If one of the dogs makes a mess on the carpet, she will clean up after it herself. After all, there are *some* things you can't ask the servants to do.

## Into the Future

WILL the monarchy survive? Norman Stone, Professor of Modern History at Oxford, is one sage who tends to regard the monarchy as a symbol of what is wrong with Britain. "All this 'ancien régimery' is looking pretty ropey," he says. "Institutions like the Church of England, the Oxford and Cambridge colleges, the House of Lords—they've all had a wonderful run, but they're in very poor condition now. I think the same applies to the monarchy. These establishments should keep up with the times or they risk becoming anachronisms."

Yet what constitutes an anachronism to an opponent like Norman

Stone becomes the "essential mystery" to a protagonist like Bishop Woods, who believes, as befits a true Christian, that there are some things which simply cannot be "rational." Their schools of thought are probably irreconcilable.

Where even the Professor has to furrow his brow is over the question, "If no monarchy, what then?" A president would almost inevitably be a less lustrous figure than the sovereign. And there is nothing about foreign presidencies, such as those of the USA, France or Germany, to suggest that a president would cost less money or preside over a country which was, in any real sense, more democratic.

The royal family still comes in for its share of criticism. At the time of the Gulf War, *The Sunday Times* ran a shrill anti-monarchist leader, suggesting that some members of the family were shirking their duty by gadding about and not lending their support to the armed forces. These strictures were deeply resented by the Palace—and also by the military, who remain conspicuously loyal to the crown.

The day after the article appeared, various members of the royal family did visit military units, but these engagements had been arranged some weeks before.

In a Gallup Poll published in *The Daily Telegraph* last July, 75 per cent of all those questioned, and 60 per cent of the under-25s, thought that the country needed a royal family.

Only 12 per cent wanted to see the monarchy abolished by the turn of the century.

In historical terms there is nothing very dramatic about these figures. As writer and historian Philip Ziegler points out, in the 50-odd years since opinion polls on the monarchy began, ten per cent or so have consistently expressed republican tendencies; in 1971, when there was a furore over the Queen's money, that figure went up to 19 per cent. Nevertheless, says Ziegler, "the danger lights are flashing."

Given the Queen's essentially conservative temperament, it seems unlikely that the institution will change dramatically while she continues to reign. She has never been prone to panic and has always listened carefully to good advice.

"She is too secure in her own judgement and in her position," as one old friend puts it, "to get fussed about the sillier campaigns run by the media."

As the years pass and the Prince of Wales moves restlessly into an apparently unfulfilled middle age, media pundits call on the Queen to make way for him, just as Queen Juliana of the Netherlands made way for her daughter Beatrix. But, as Lord Charteris told me: "Abdication is a dirty word."

The Queen Mother never forgave her brother-in-law, Edward VIII, for quitting his post, and the Queen's view is that once anointed with the holy oil at her Coronation she has a solemn obligation never to renounce her title or her role. Abdication is a subject she has discussed informally with advisers, but any formal mention of it to the Palace elicits an official denial that the Queen is considering it.

The sovereign and the monarchy have lived through 40 years of almost constant change in every area, and they have managed to accommodate it while remaining beacons of constancy in an uncertain world. "I wouldn't claim that the monarchy has prevented a Red revolution," says Lord Charteris. "But it has been a steadying influence on the nation. And despite everything, it has managed to retain enough of its mystery and its majesty."

Shortly after the 1991 royal visit to the USA, James Orr commented on the Queen's address to the American Congress: "The expressions on the faces of those hardbitten Congressmen and Senators were such that they might have been applauding a saint."

The special relationship between the Queen and her peoples and the rest of the world is unquestionably mysterious and ultimately inexplicable. But, against all odds, it remains intact. The achievement is undeniable. **THE END**

*A major exhibition, "Sovereign," celebrating the Queen's 40-year reign opens at London's Victoria and Albert Museum in April and runs until September.*

*Queen Elizabeth addressing the American Congress in 1991,*
*watched by Vice President Dan Quayle (rear left)*

# A Royal Commission

BY RUSSELL TWISK, EDITOR-IN-CHIEF

W HEN I asked the artist Tai-Shan Schierenberg to my office in 1995 he was intrigued by the secrecy surrounding my invitation. All I told him was that I was keen to commission a painting of "two very distinguished people".

I had looked at the work of many young artists but I had been particularly impressed by Schierenberg's powerful portrait of the writer and barrister John Mortimer, which hangs in the National Portrait Gallery. Now 35, Schierenberg—who was born in Skegness and has a Chinese mother and German father, also a painter—came to prominence in 1989 when he won the John Player Portrait Award with a painting of his wife, artist Lynn Dennison.

His curiosity was replaced by stunned silence when I told him that Reader's Digest wanted him to paint a portrait of the Queen and Prince Philip to celebrate the couple's Golden

*Tai-Shan Schierenberg in his studio*

Wedding anniversary on November 20 this year.

The Queen was "delighted" with the idea. In 1986 we had commissioned a portrait by Michael Leonard to celebrate her sixtieth birthday. Today it is one of the National Portrait Gallery's most popular pictures, and is known affectionately as "Corgi and Bess".

Her Majesty asked if this new portrait—only the second time she and the Duke had posed together—could be painted at Windsor, a favourite official residence.

Schierenberg was aware his most demanding commission was double-edged. It was bound to enhance his reputation, but all royal portraits are controversial.

He arrived at Windsor a year later for the initial photo session, and arranged the furniture in the Oak Room of the private apartments so the couple could be seen against a window with the

*Her Majesty The Queen and His Royal Highness The Duke of Edinburgh*
by TAI-SHAN SCHIERENBERG
Commissioned for their Golden Wedding Anniversary,
November 20, 1997, by Reader's Digest

Round Tower in the background.

The Duke arrived and suggested that it would be far better if he sat on the window-seat rather than on the sofa. The Queen then pitched in to help Schierenberg and his photographer move the lighting and furniture around for the composition.

This informality was the first of many surprises for the artist, who worked at both Windsor and Buckingham Palace when busy royal diaries meant that he had to paint the couple separately.

Prince Philip, a keen amateur artist, chatted with Schierenberg about different ways to paint skies, then took him on a tour of his private collection at Windsor. On completing a sitting with the Queen at Buckingham Palace, Schierenberg was left to view some of the priceless paintings that line the corridors.

"I drove my wife mad, coming back after each sitting and telling her how natural and charming and amusing the Queen was," he recalls.

Back in his small studio, above an office in Notting Hill Gate, and surrounded by hundreds of photos and sketches, Schierenberg began four months' work on his huge canvas which measures six feet by five.

He struggled, as he always does, wiping out work that didn't satisfy him. "It is not until the fourth or fifth attempt at painting a subject that I feel I may have begun to capture their real

*Tai-Shan Schierenberg at the unveiling of his portrait of John Mortimer at the National Portrait Gallery in London, 1992*

essence as people. I'm always striving for that magic moment when paint becomes an illusion of reality."

In Schierenberg's portrayal of the royal couple, with its dramatic use of thickly applied paint, the artist breaks with convention. He explains: "The light coming from behind them makes us, the viewers, the observed ones, rather than them being the observed people."

Some may find the couple's hands disconcerting. "I always seem to paint hands larger than they are," Schierenberg admits. "It makes the painting slightly more monumental."

To me this exciting portrait, which features on our back cover this month, is a tremendously powerful, honest image of a couple who have come through much but remain steadfastly together.

In a year dominated by the tragic death of Diana, Princess of Wales, when the Royal Family has had to weather stinging criticism, it is apt that the Queen and Prince Philip are seen at Windsor. The sumptuous state apartments destroyed or damaged by fire in 1992 have been fully restored, mainly funded by entry charges to the Castle Precincts and state apartments at Buckingham Palace. They are to reopen to the public at the end of this year—a symbol of our monarchy's ability to adapt and renew itself. ■

PHOTOGRAPH: © GAUTIER DEBLONDE

## *Quotable Quotes*

LET US not look back in anger, nor forward in fear, but around in awareness.
—James Thurber, *Credos and Curios*
(Hamish Hamilton)

NOTHING promotes happiness like substituting work for worry.
—Maurice Maeterlinck

WOMEN are most fascinating between the ages of 35 and 40, after they have won a few races and know how to pace themselves. Since few women ever pass 40, maximum fascination can continue indefinitely.
—Christian Dior

A PLAY is fiction—and fiction is fact distorted into truth.
—Edward Albee

IN DEPLORING the state of the world, perhaps we expect too much of the human race too soon. On dark days, it is worth remembering that the word "civilization" itself was coined by a Frenchman only 200 years ago.
—Sydney Harris

THERE is no one less fortunate than he whom adversity neglects: he has no chance to prove himself. · —Seneca

**Project Editor** Jo Bourne
**Senior Art Editor** Conorde Clarke
**Designers** Sailesh Patel, Chris Francis
**Research Assistant** Madeline Allen

FOR VIVAT DIRECT
**Editorial Director** Julian Browne
**Art Director** Anne-Marie Bulat
**Managing Editor** Nina Hathway
**Trade Books Editor** Penny Craig
**Picture Resource Manager** Sarah Stewart-Richardson
**Pre-press Account Manager** Dean Russell
**Product Production Manager** Claudette Bramble
**Production Controller** Jan Bucil

Origination by FMG
Printed in China

ISBN 978 1 78020 100 9
Book Code 400-579 UP0000-1